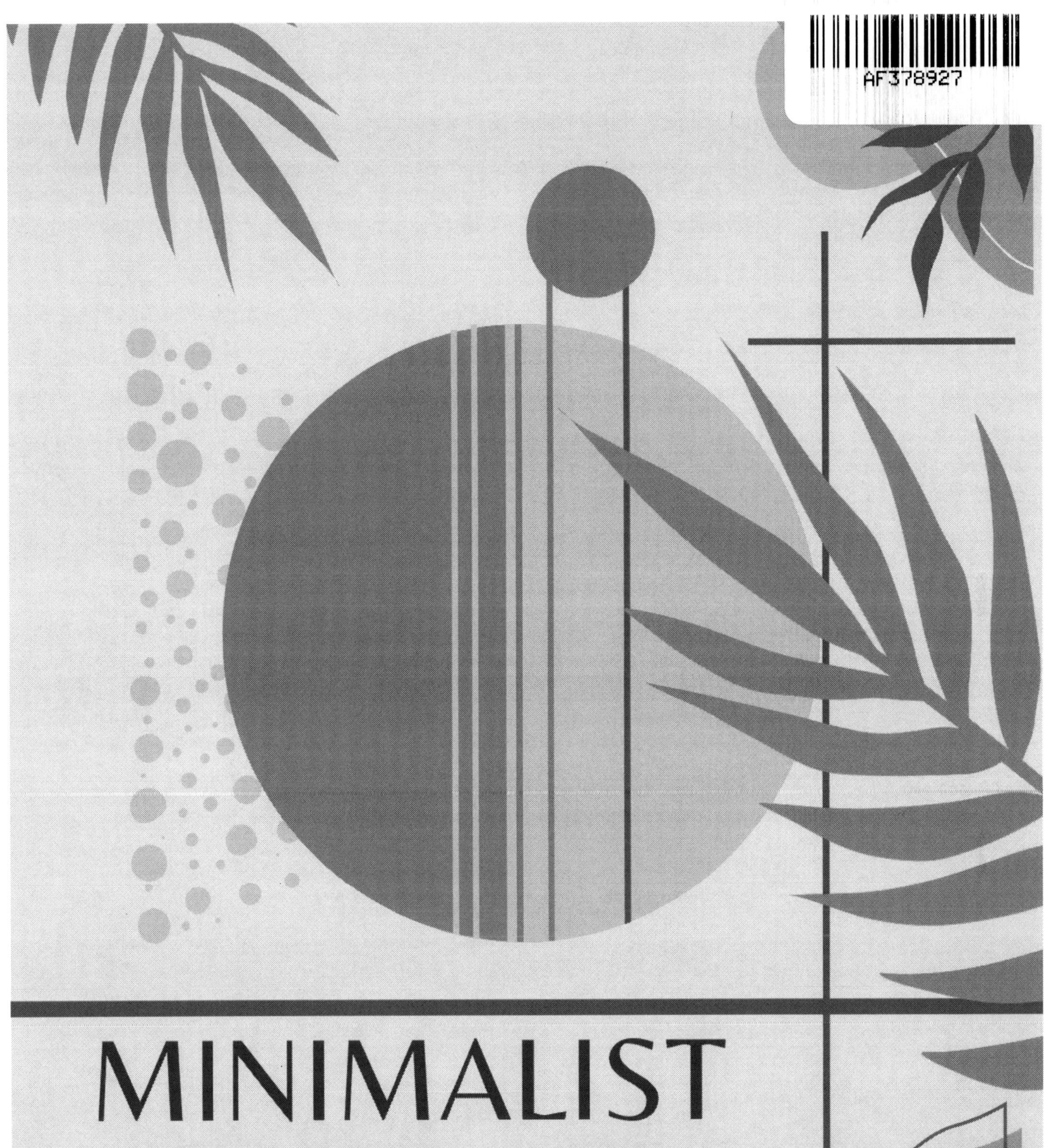

MINIMALIST BOHO ART

Coloring Book

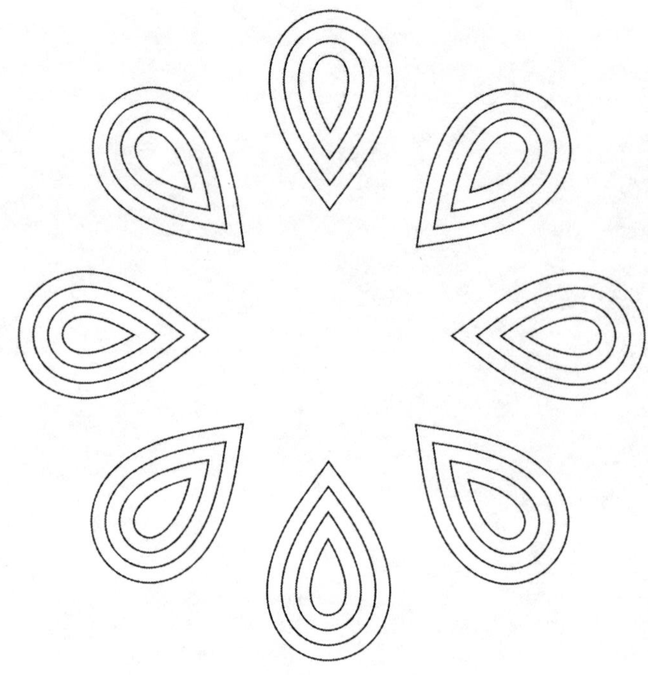

ISBN: 9781960924025

Thank you for purchasing To the Tea Prints Minimalist Boho Art Coloring Book!

This coloring book contains 40 modern and abstract pages to help unwind and release creativity. A friendly tip: to help eliminate bleed-through from certain coloring tools place a piece of paper between pages.

We hope you enjoy engaging your brain and nourishing your soul while using this book. Your support allows us to continue following our dreams and creating! We greatly appreciate your feedback and know you have many choices among talented artists. We aim to create more coloring books in the future. Let us know what you would like to see by connecting with us on social media or at *communications@totheteaprints.com*

Wishing you everything and the best,

– To the Tea Prints

We value seeing your creations!
Share your work. 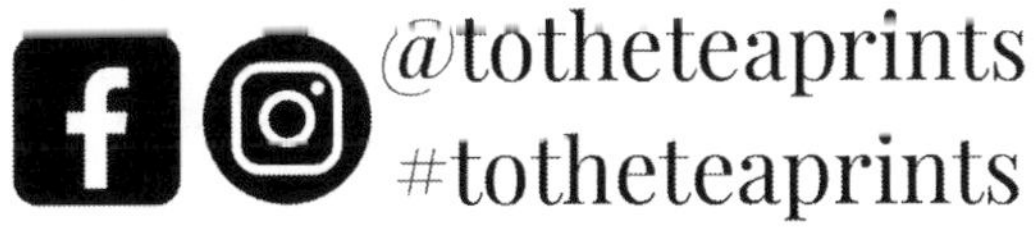

f 🅞 @totheteaprints
#totheteaprints

To the Tea
PRINTS

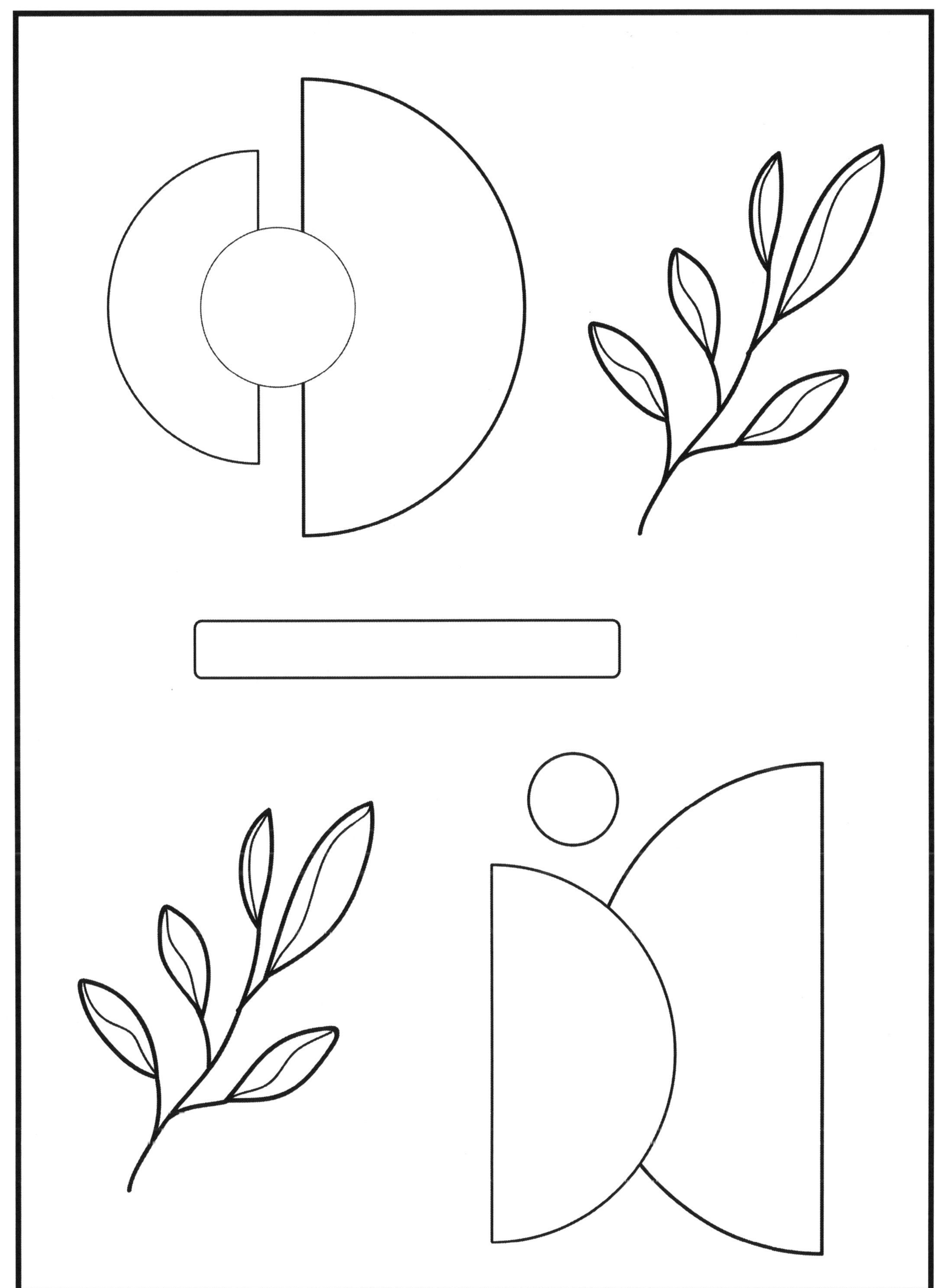

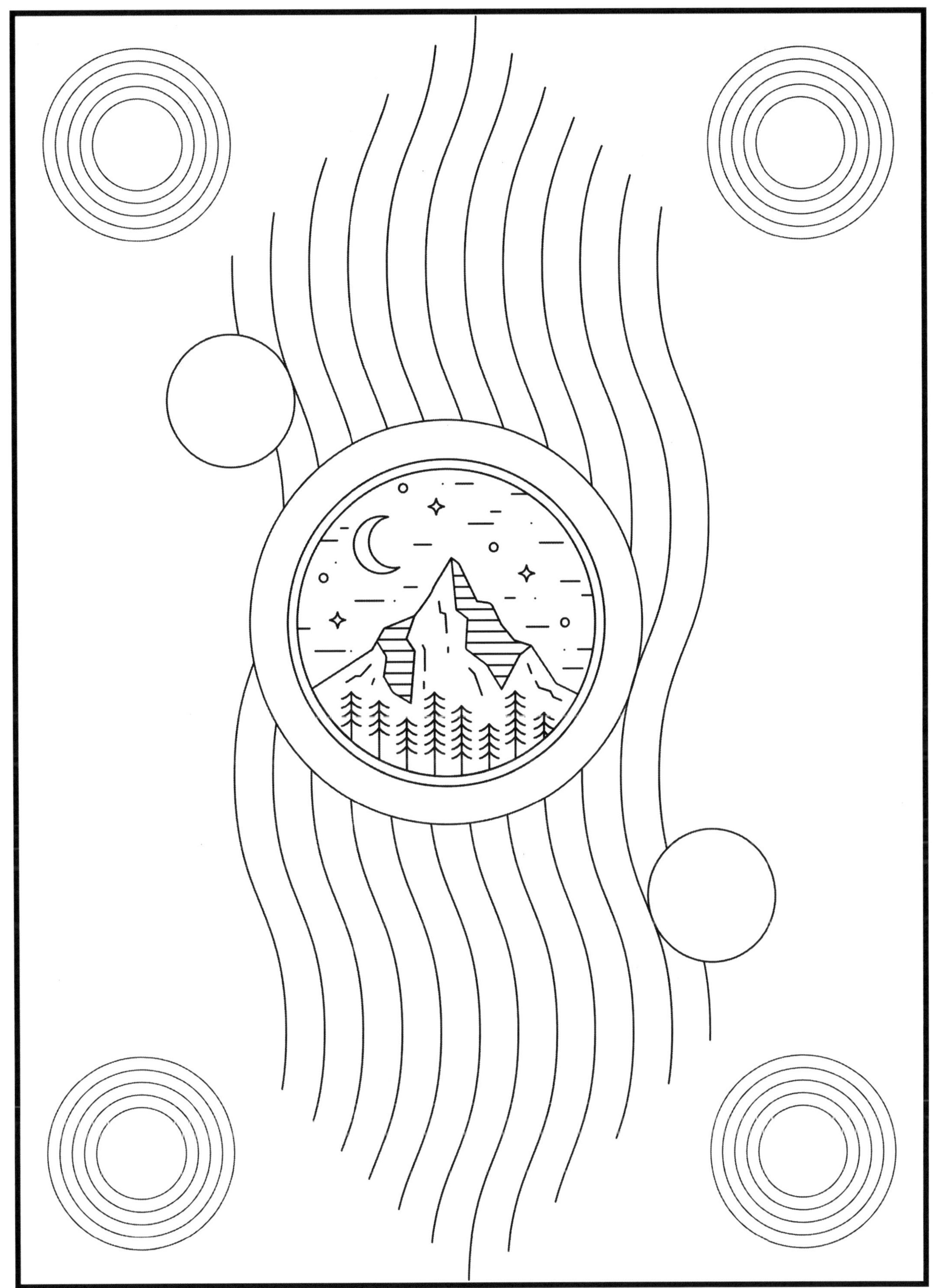

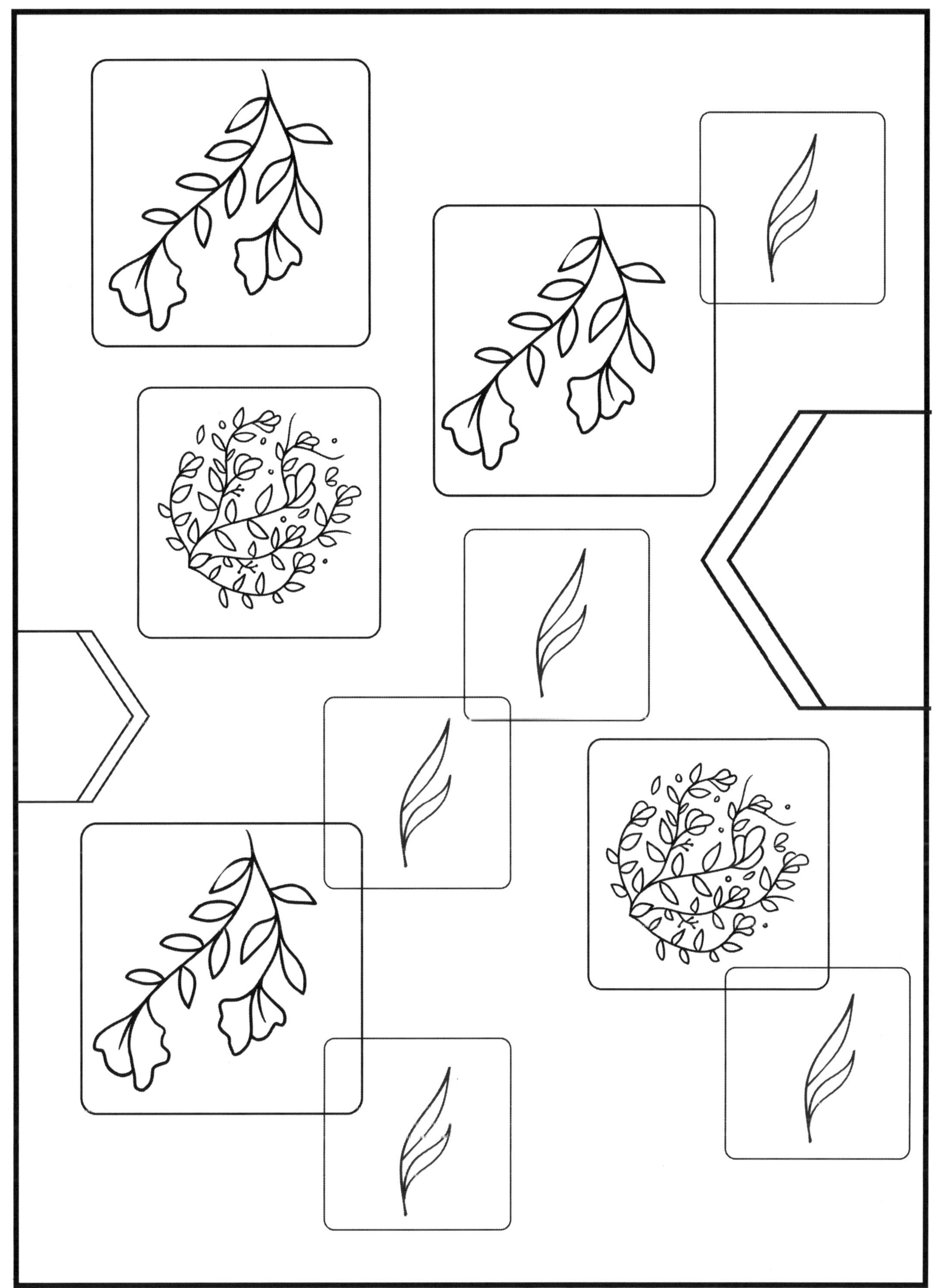

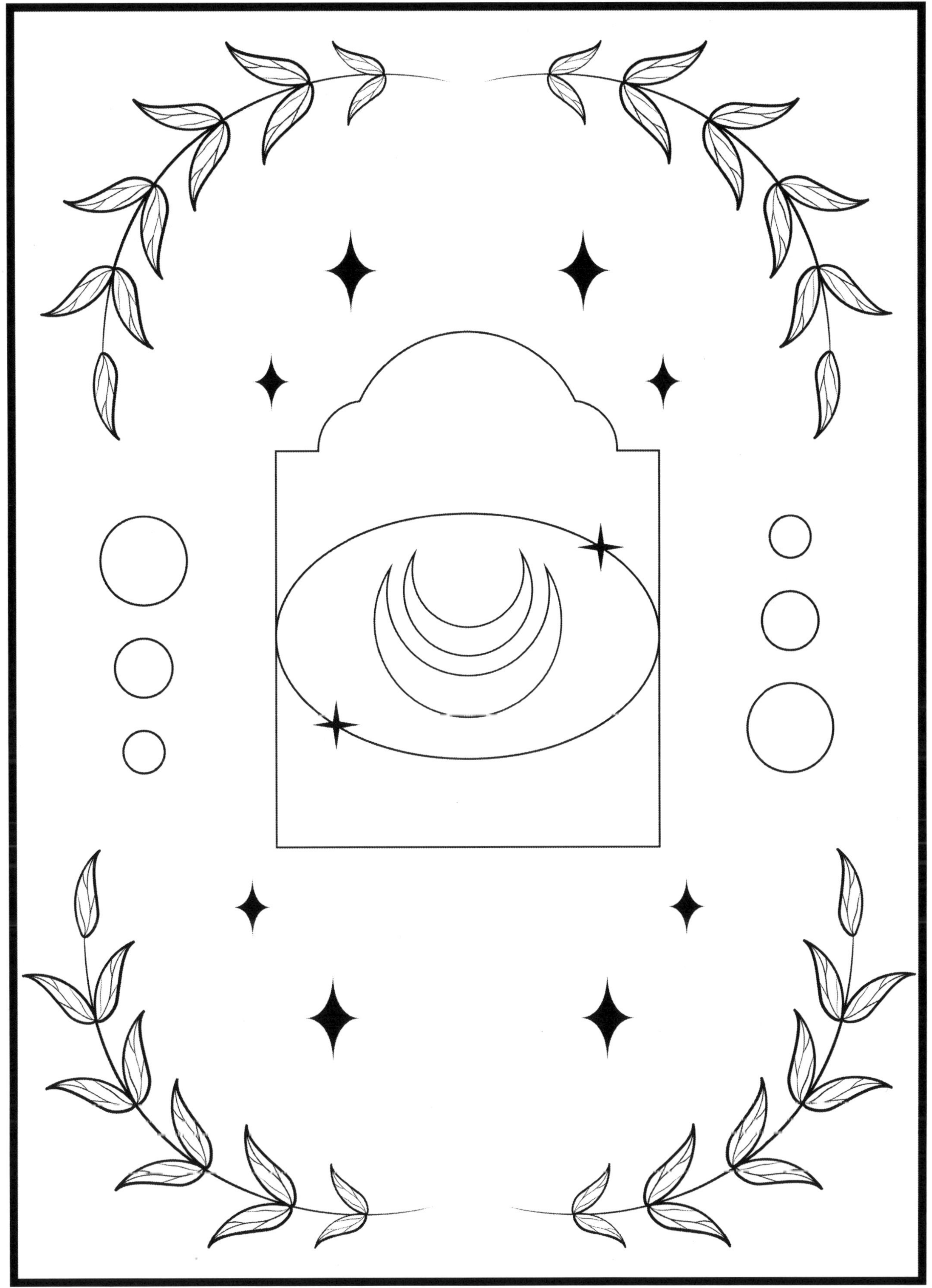

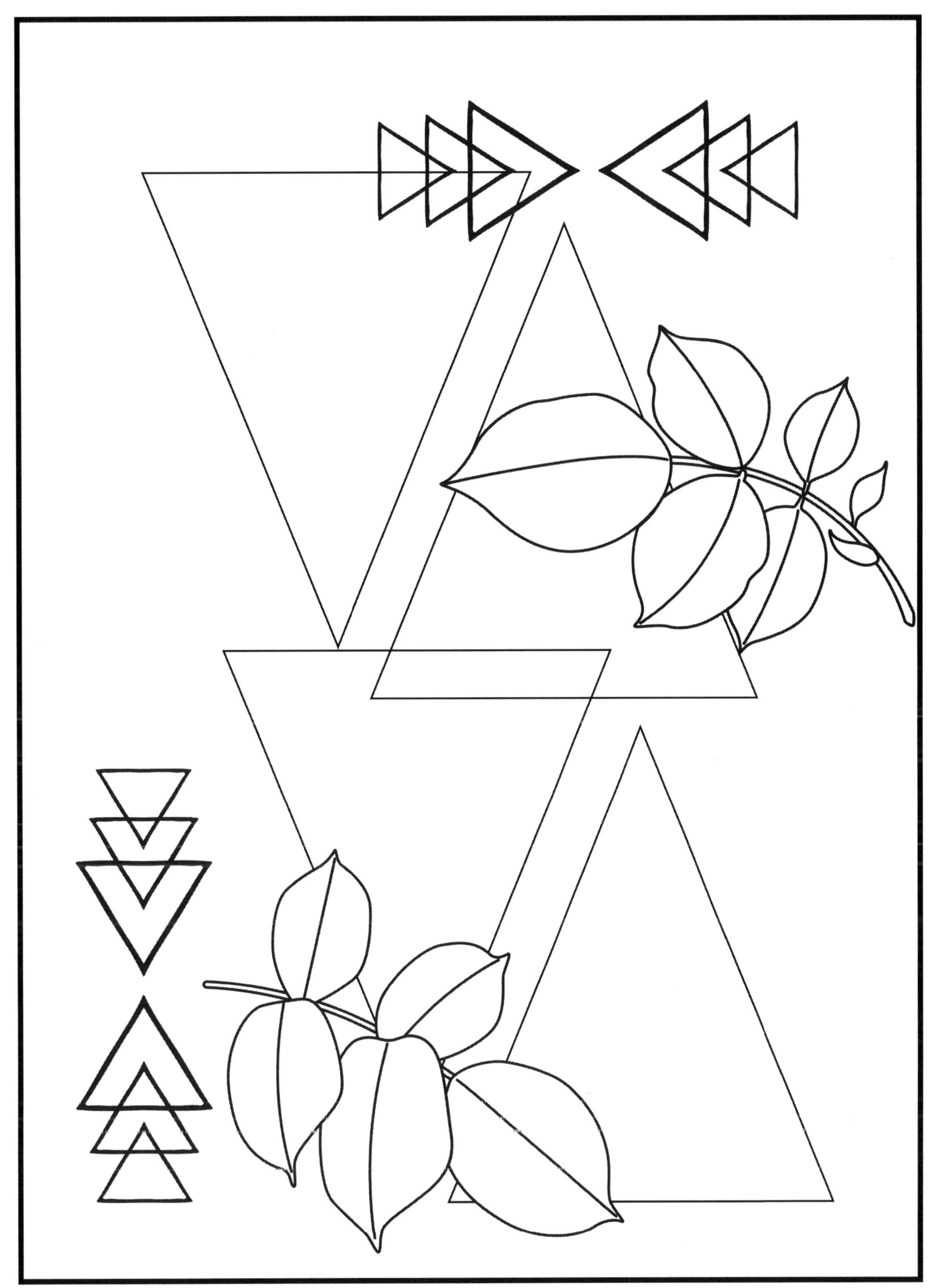

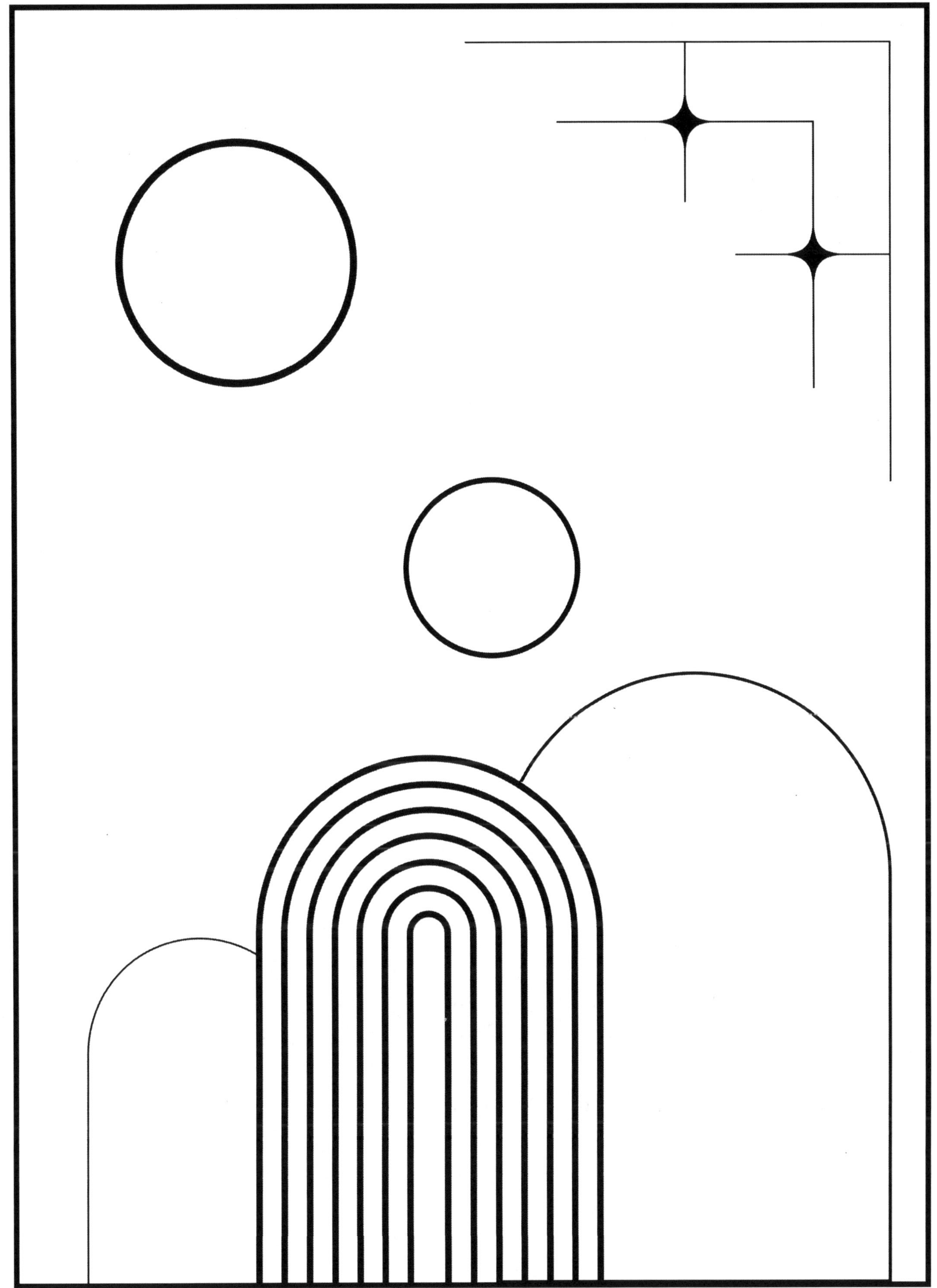

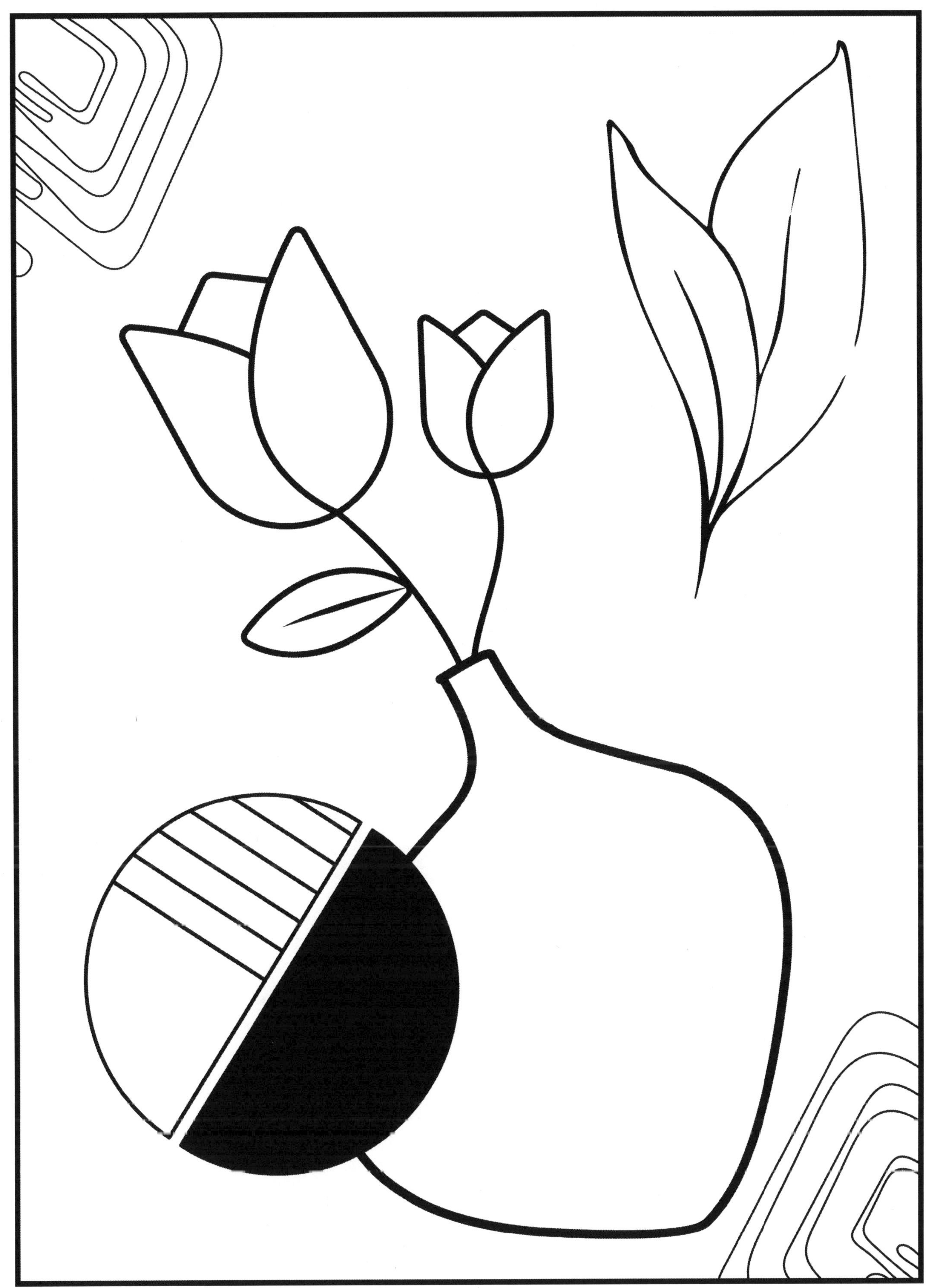

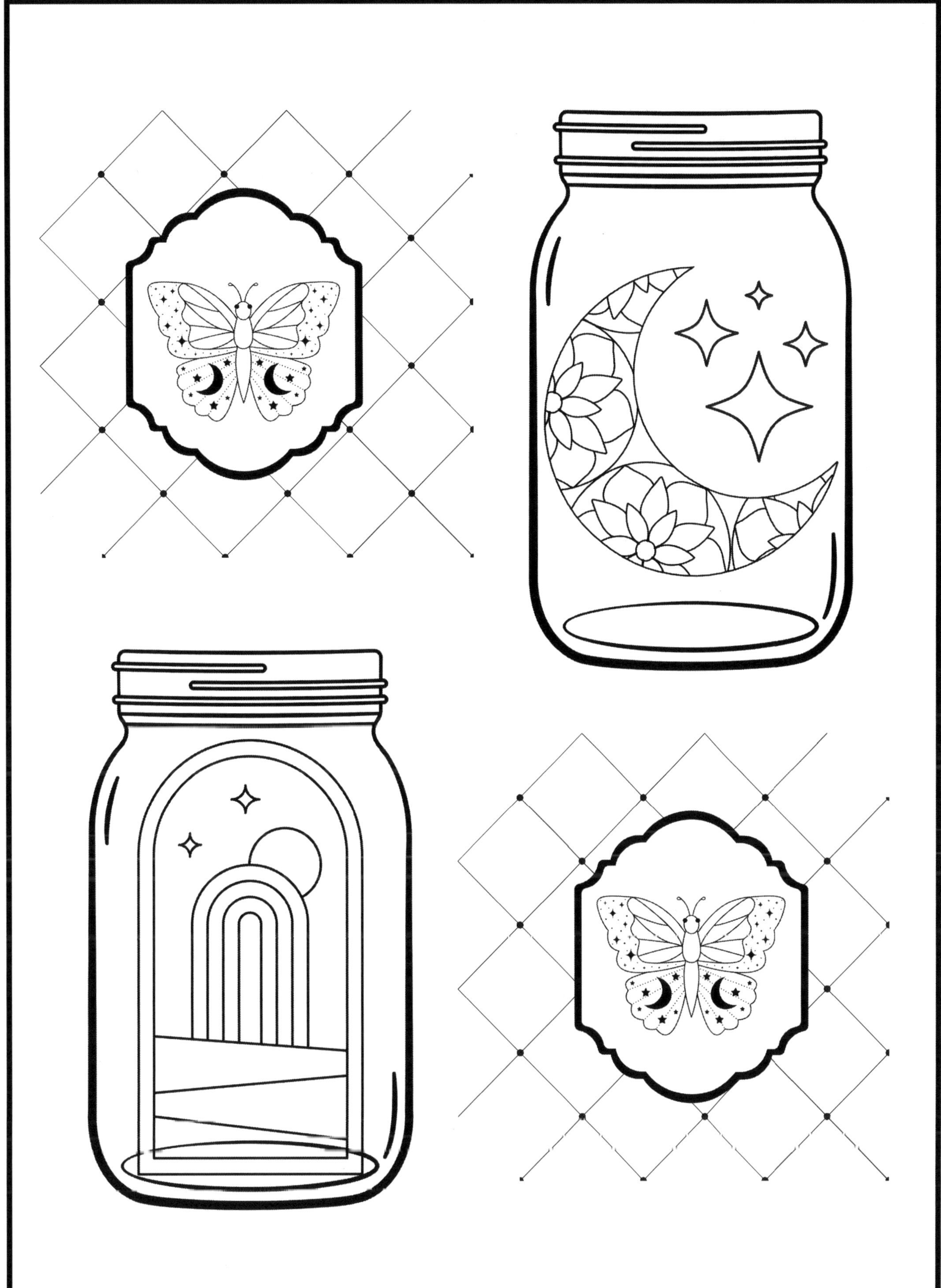

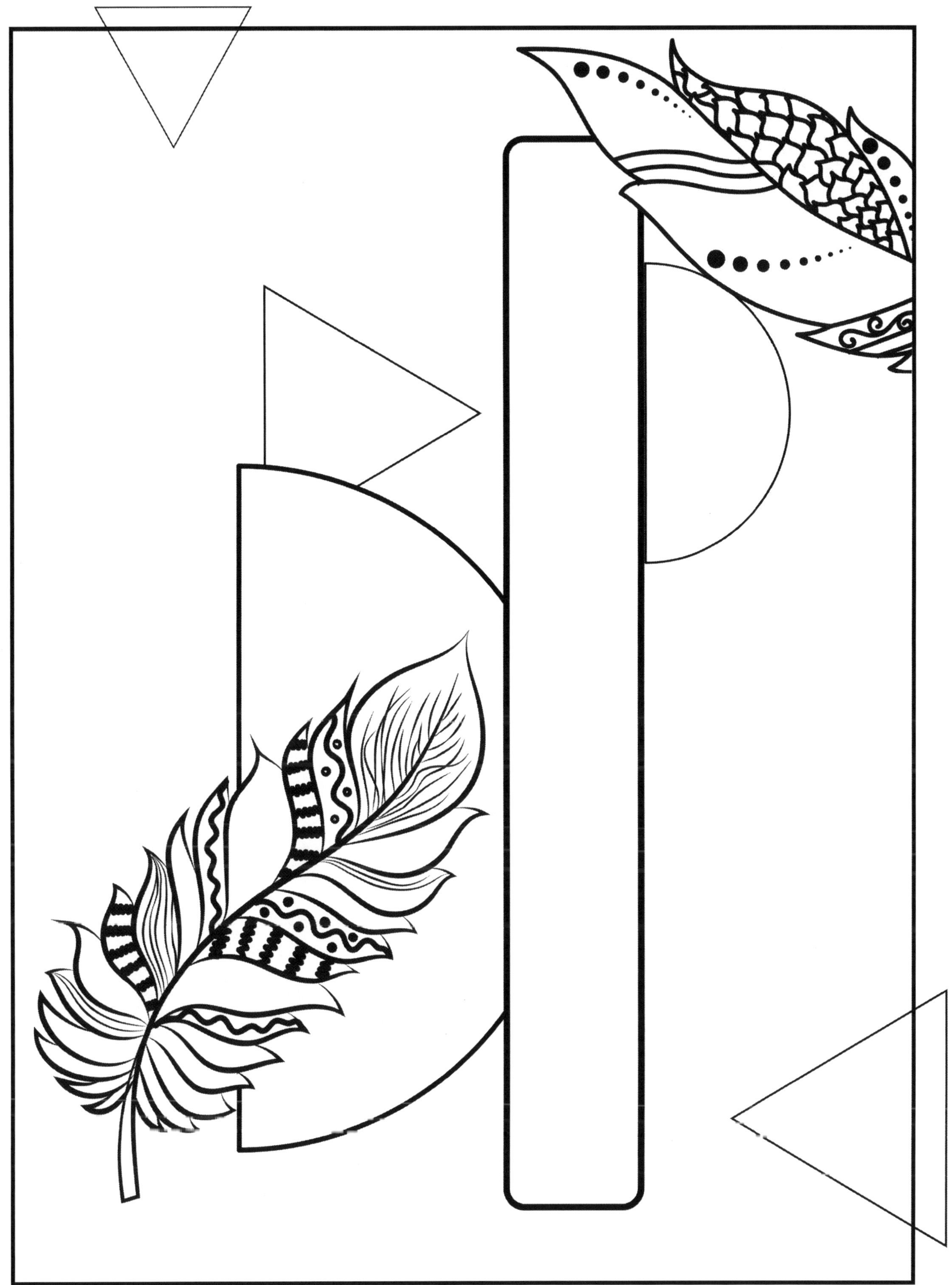

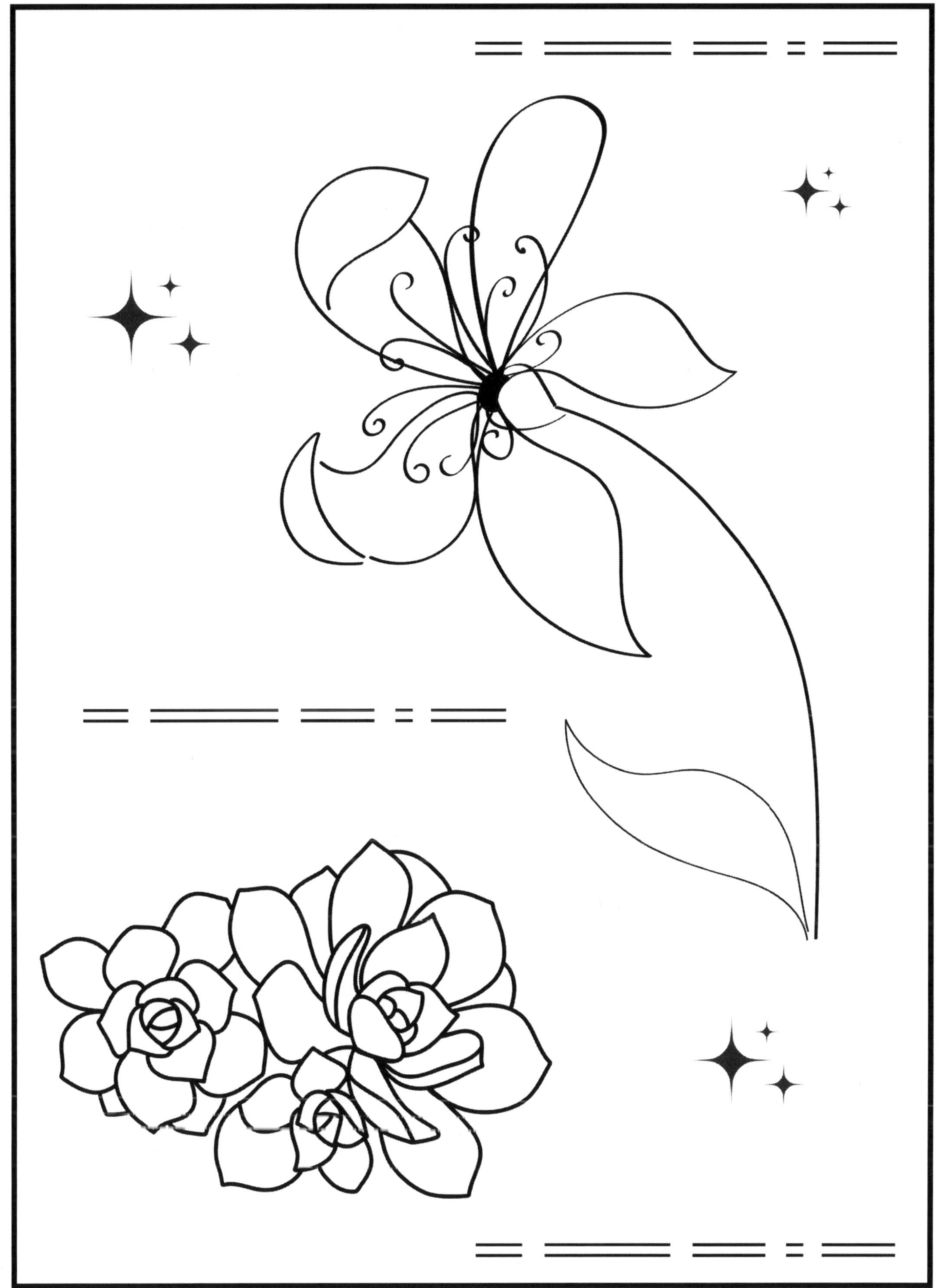

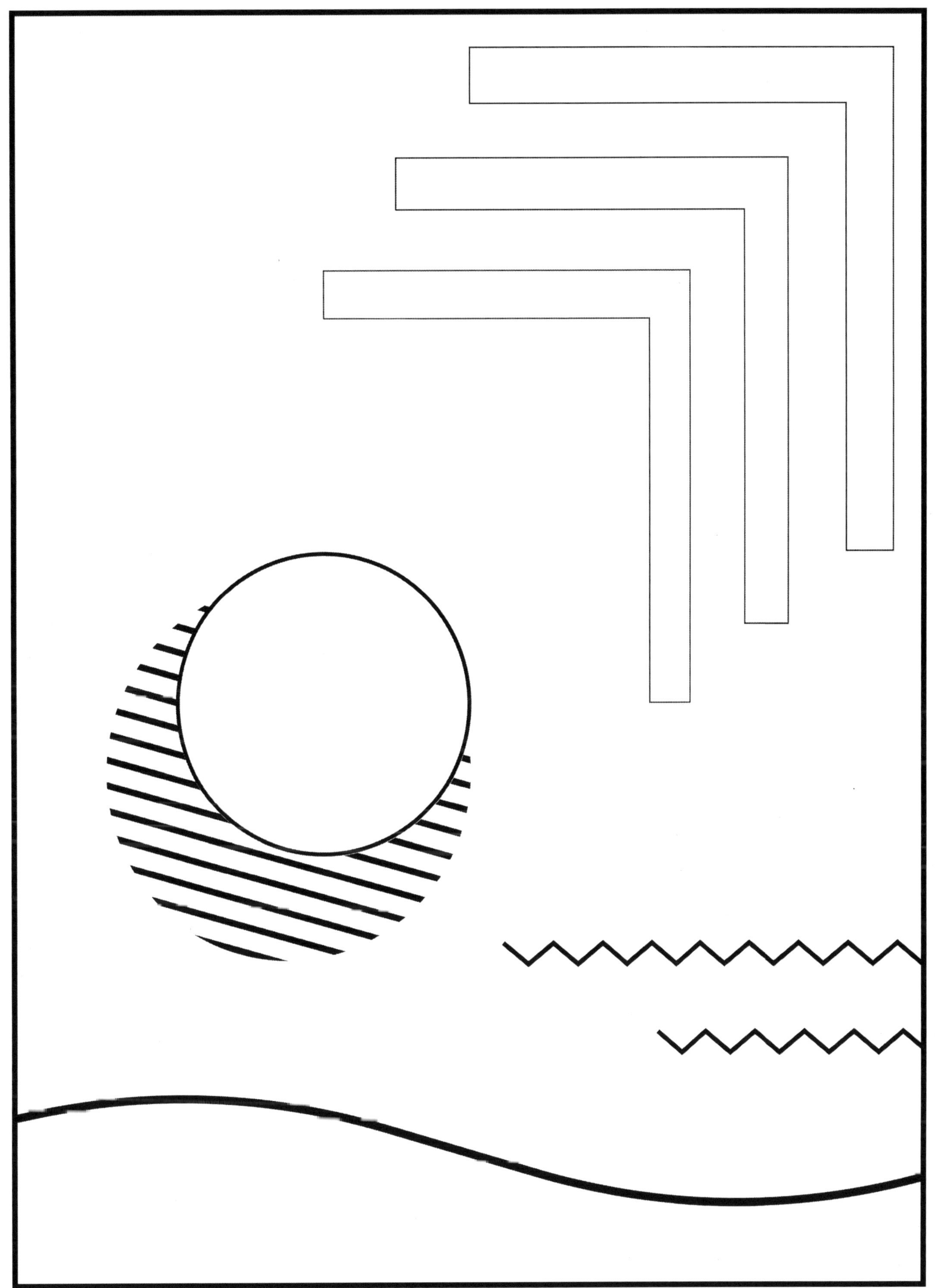

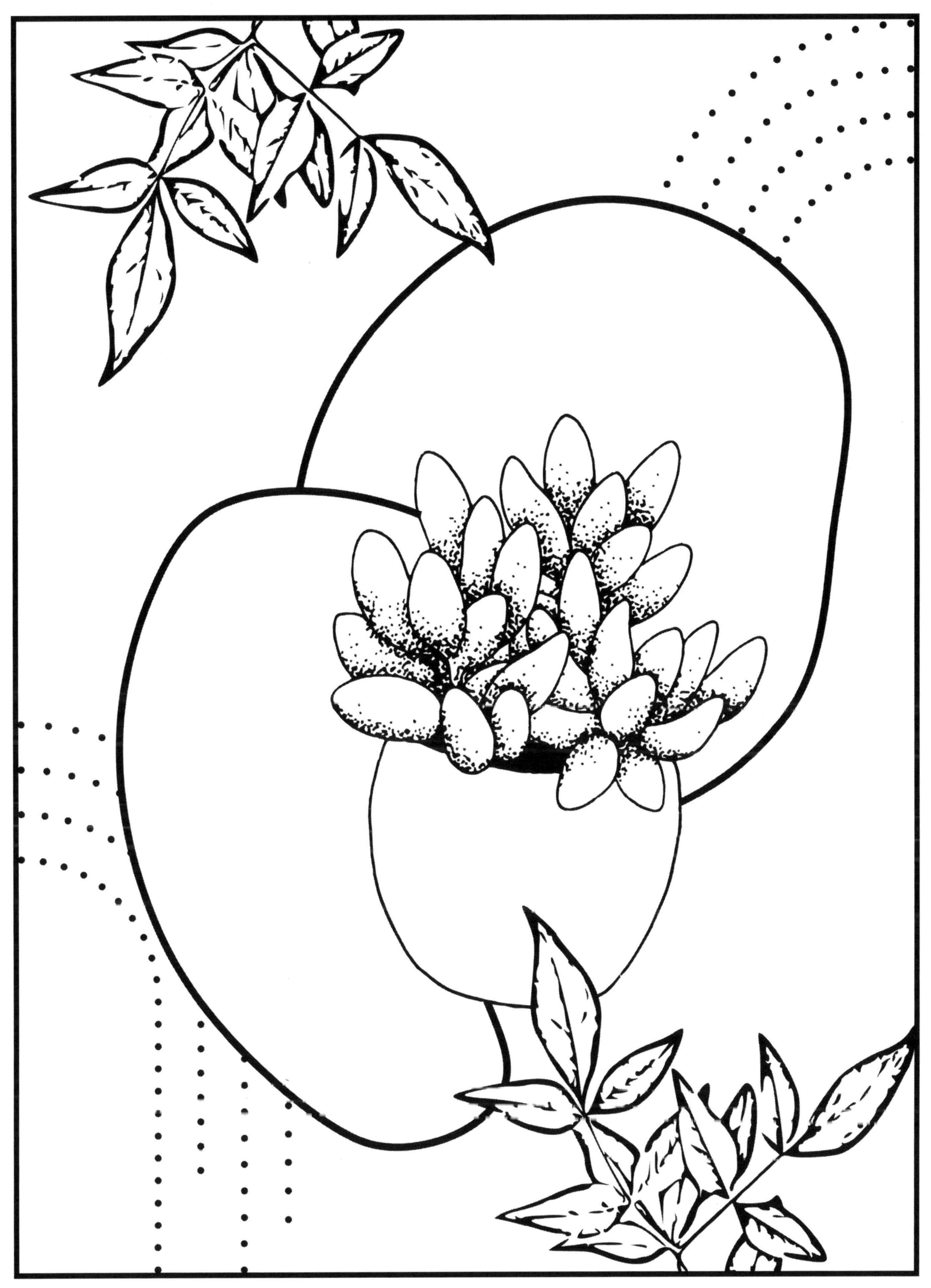

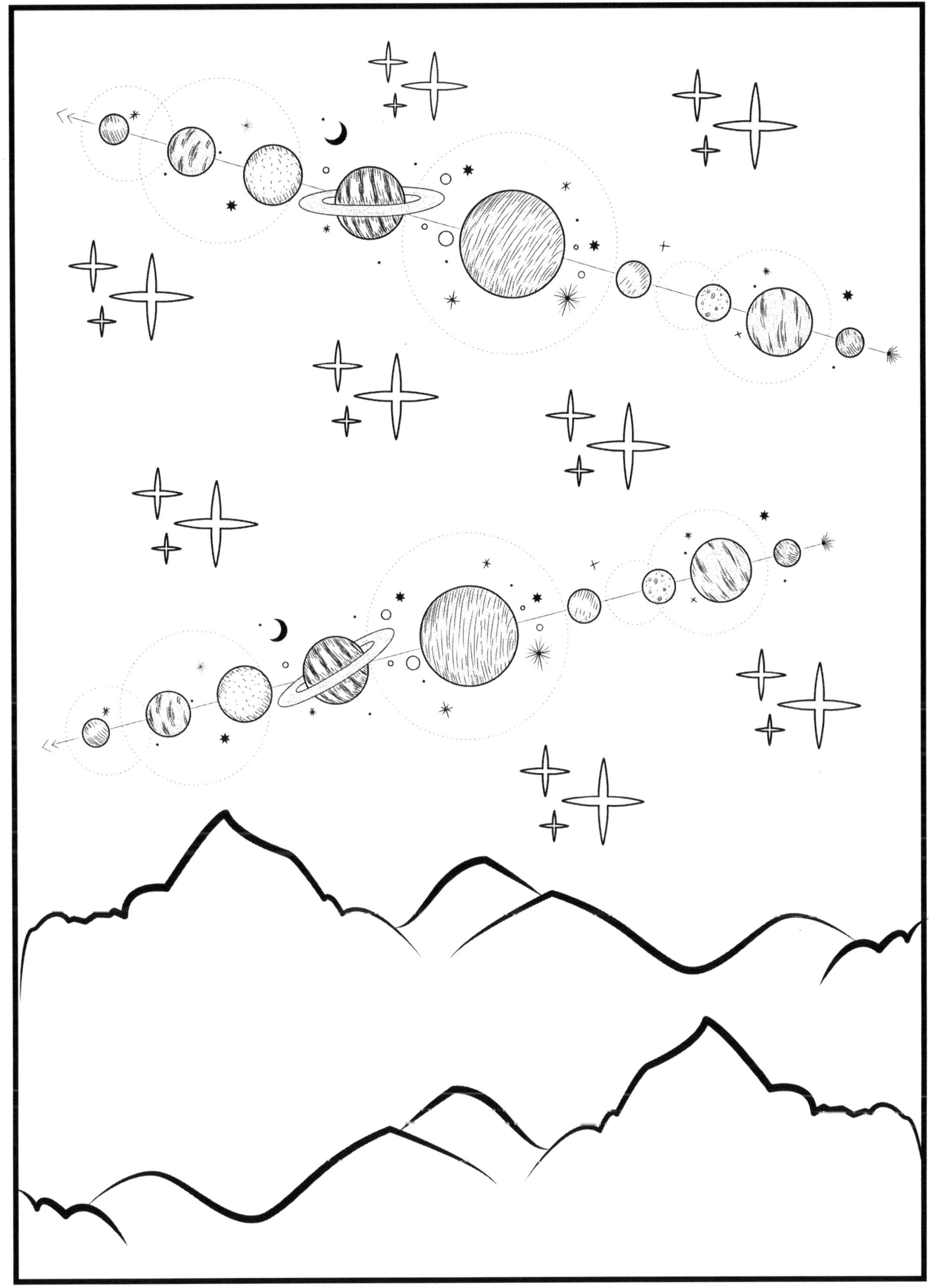

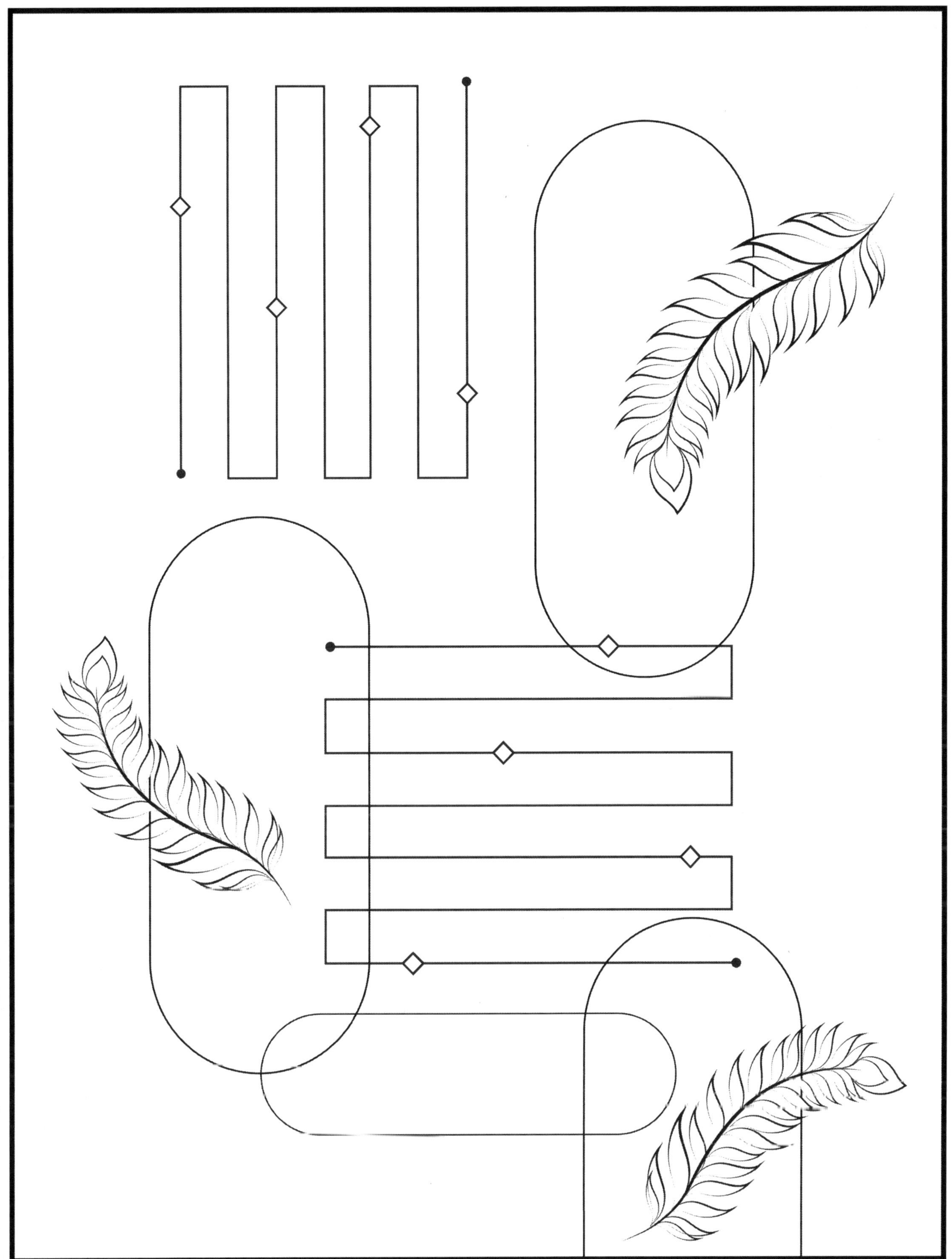

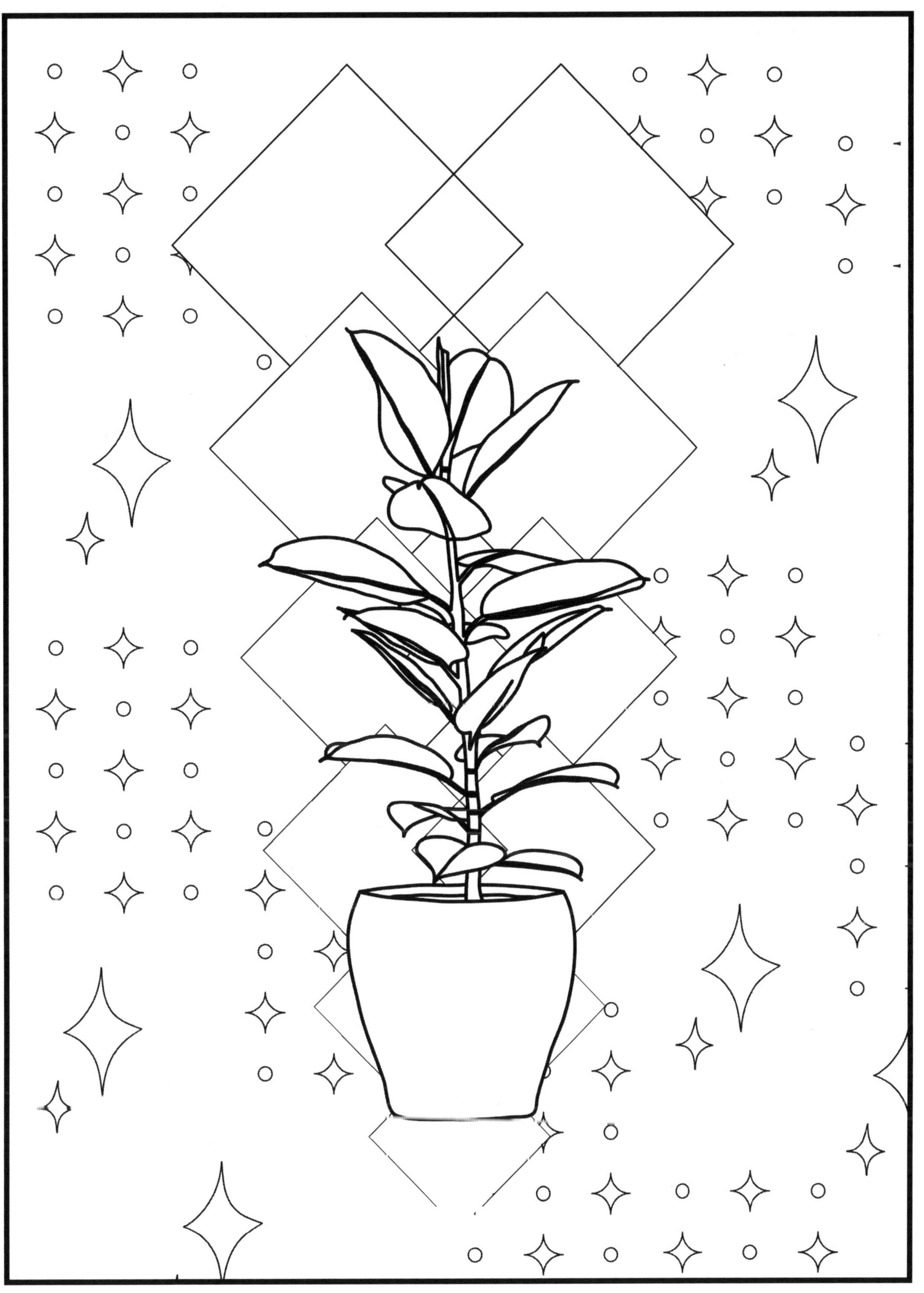

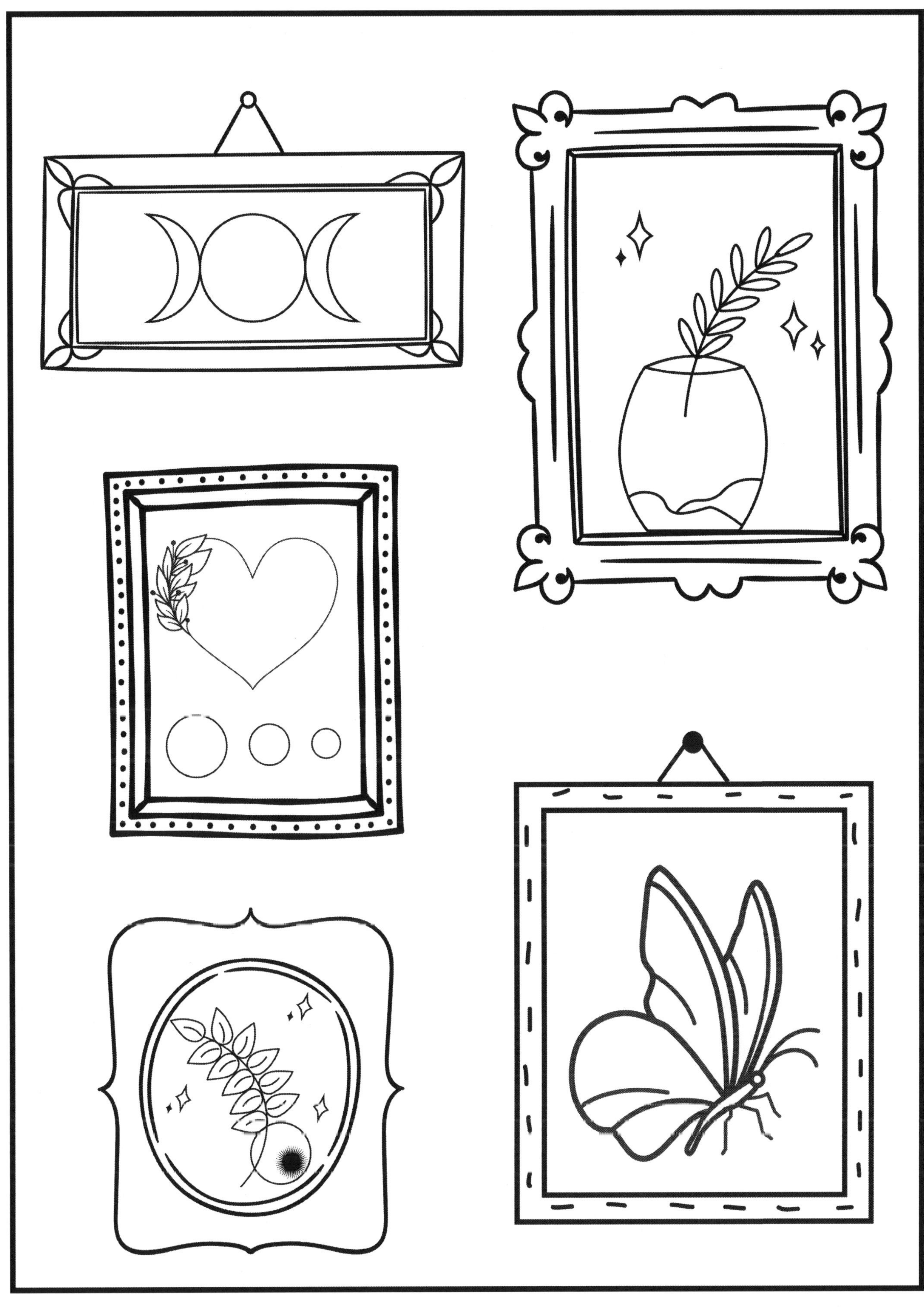

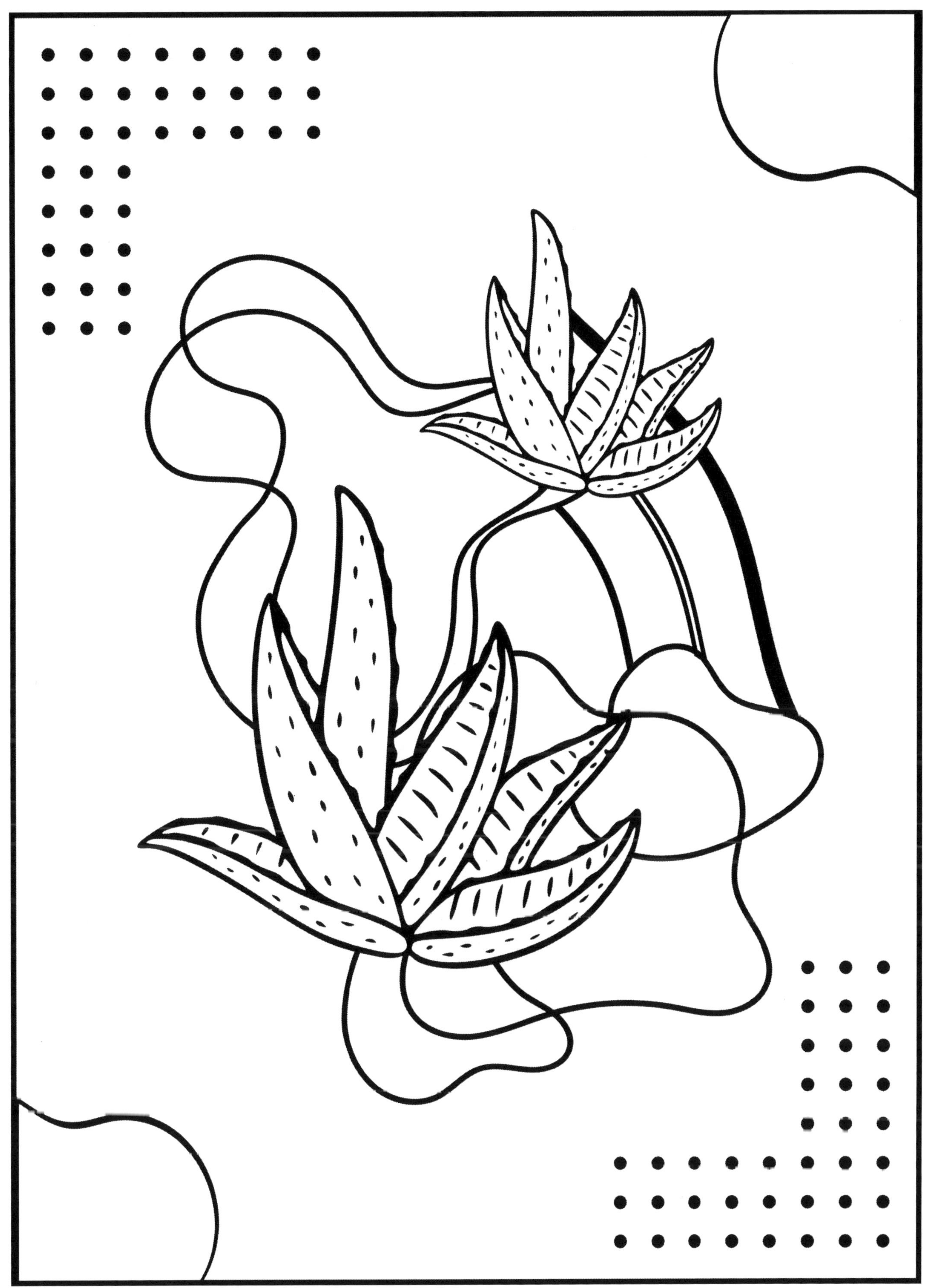

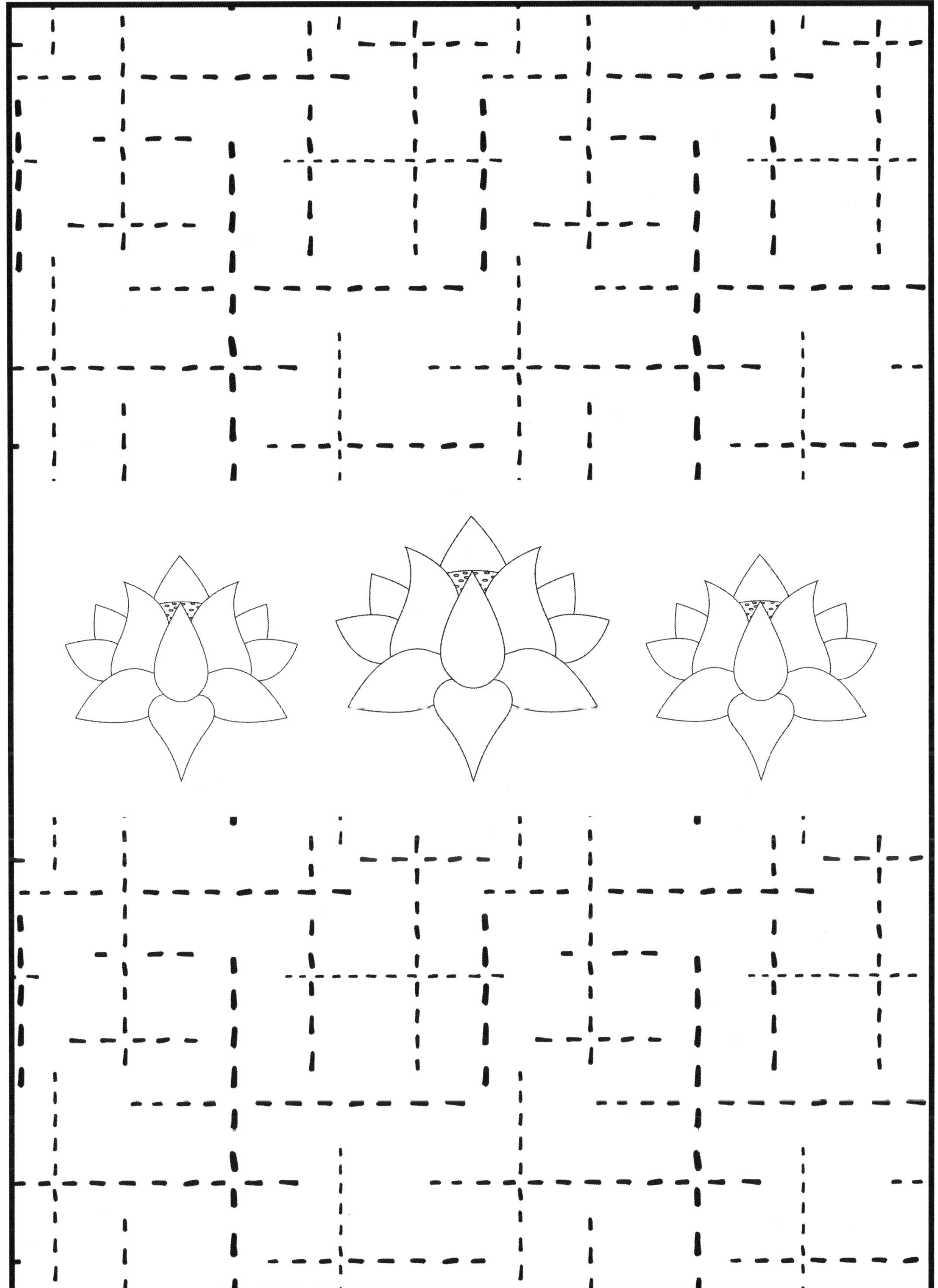

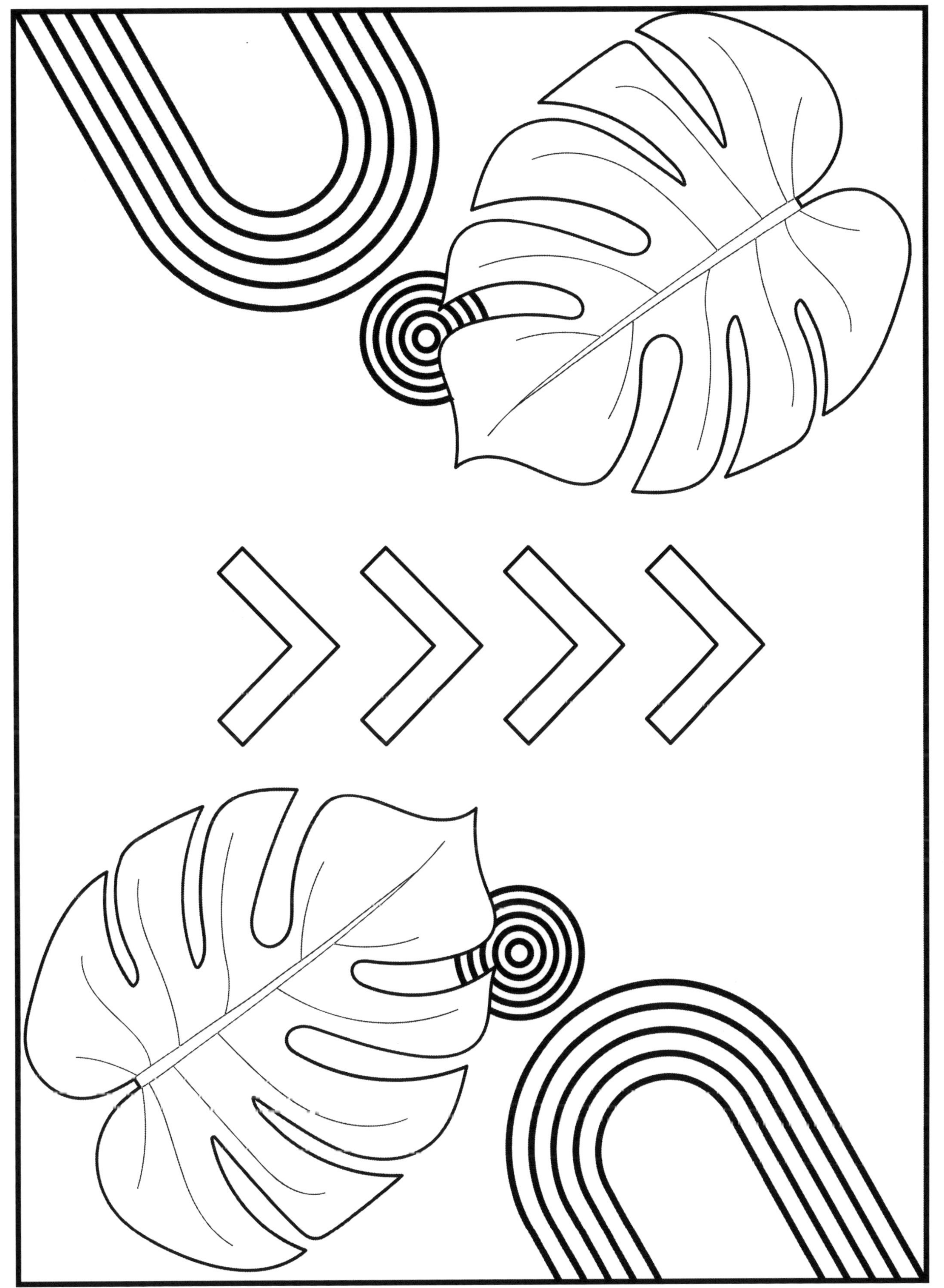

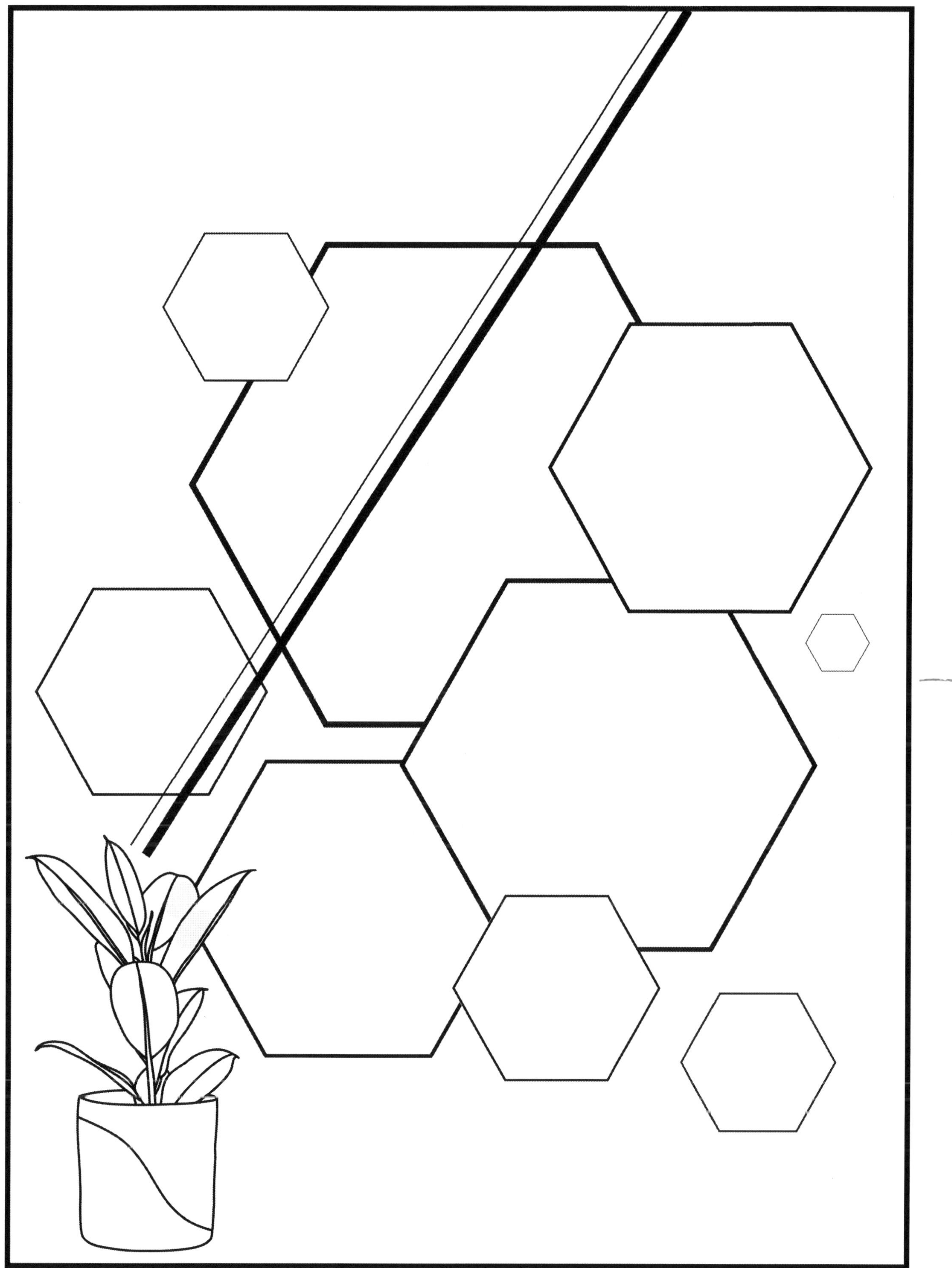

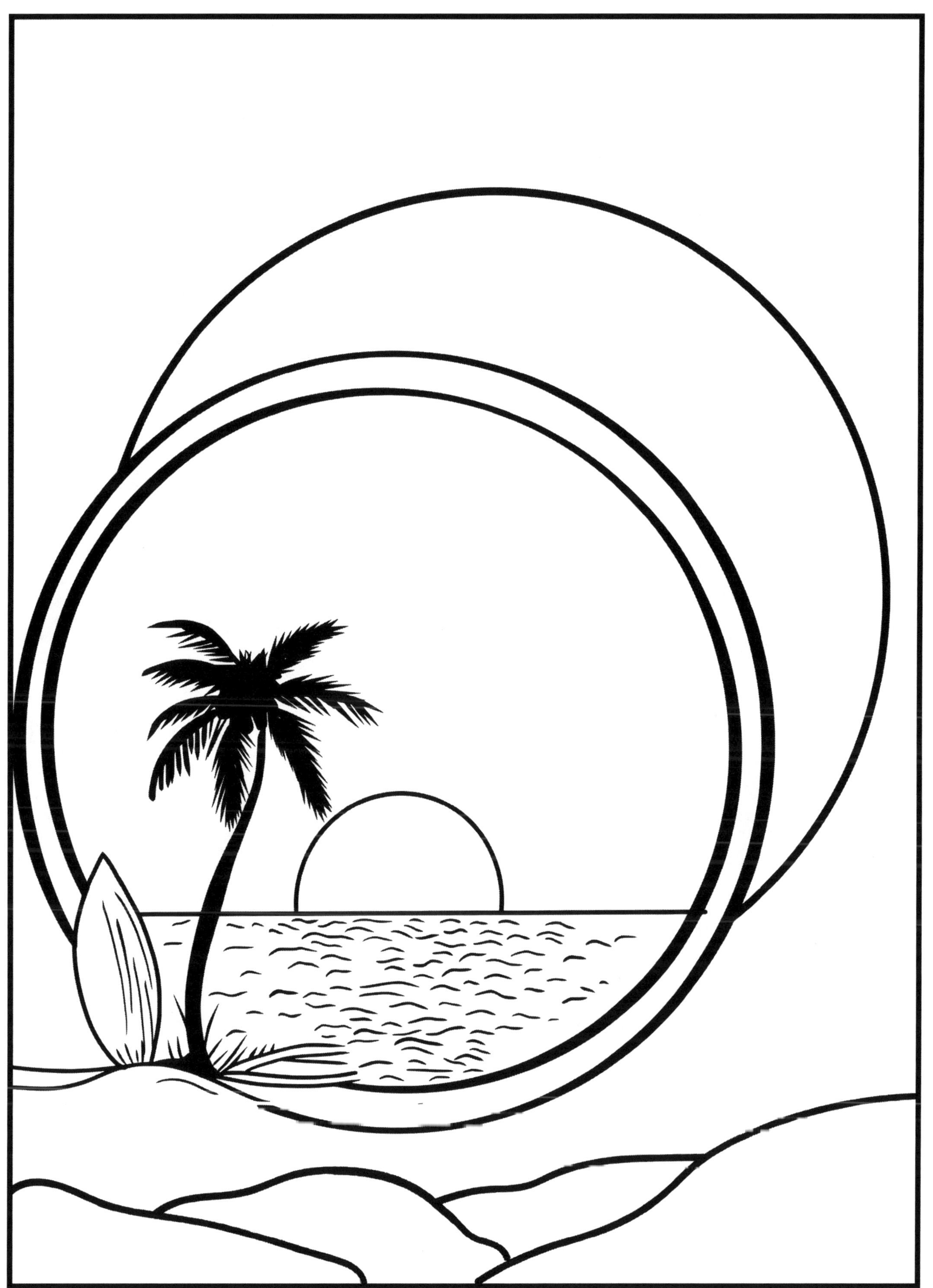

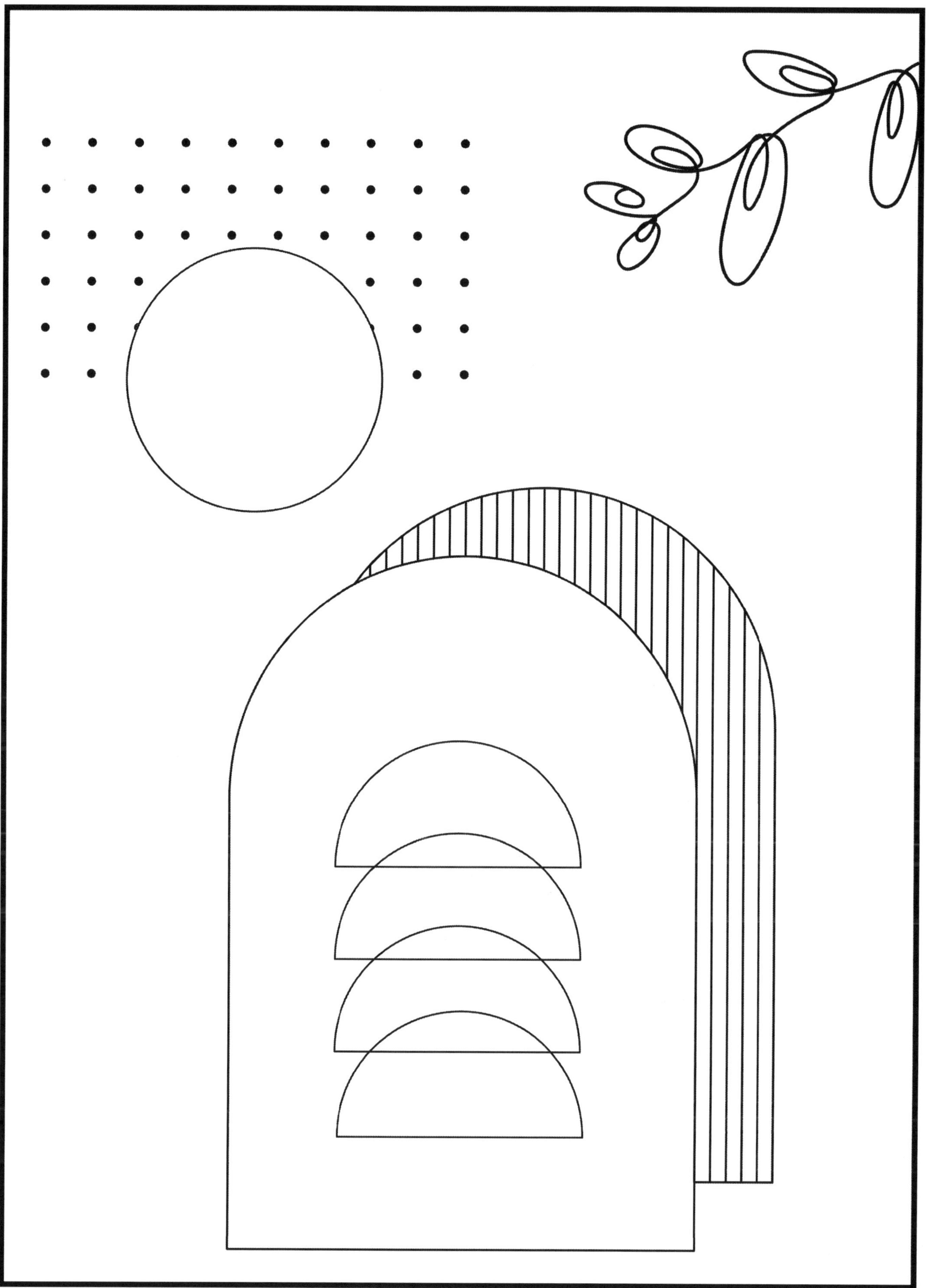

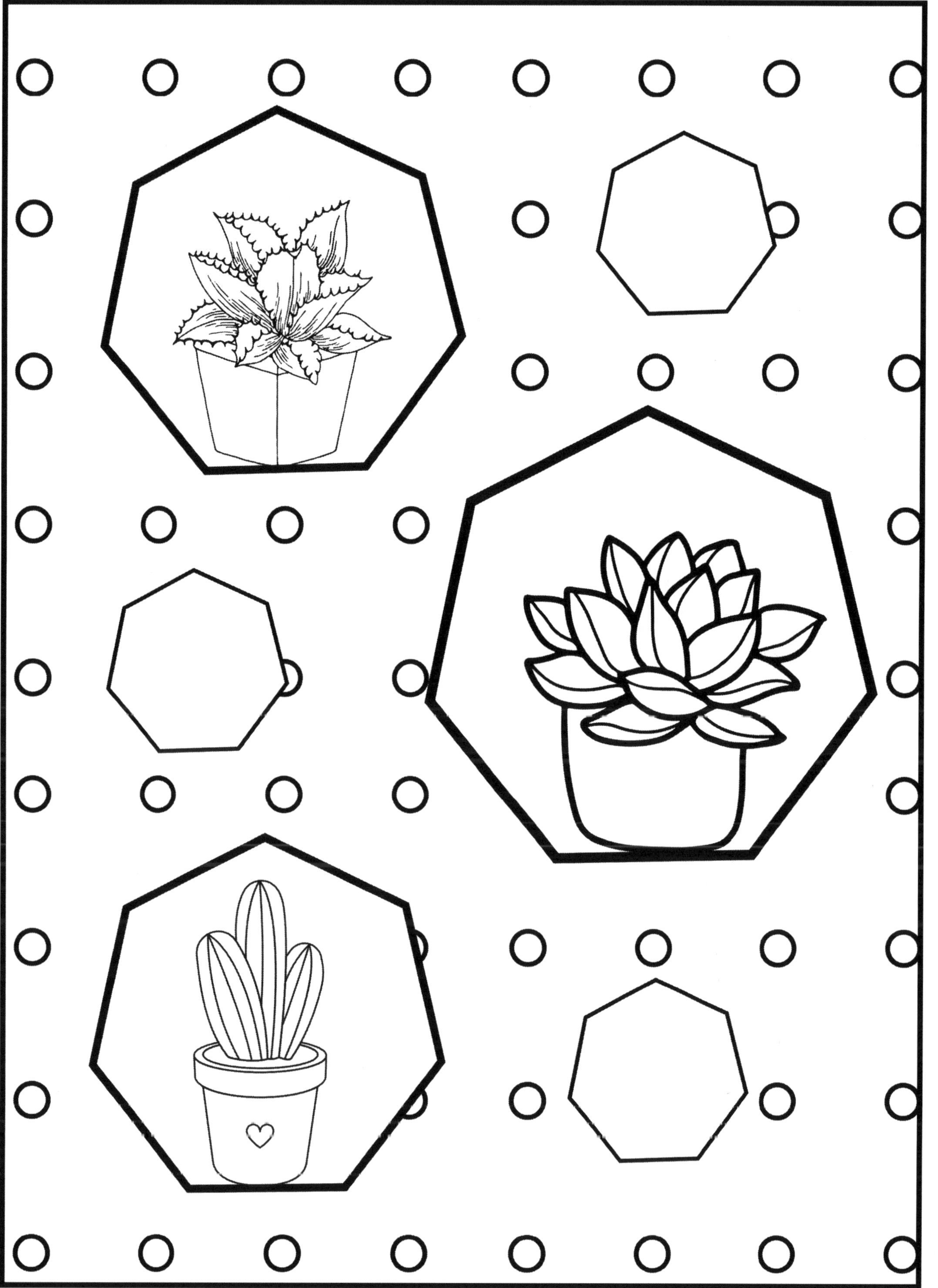

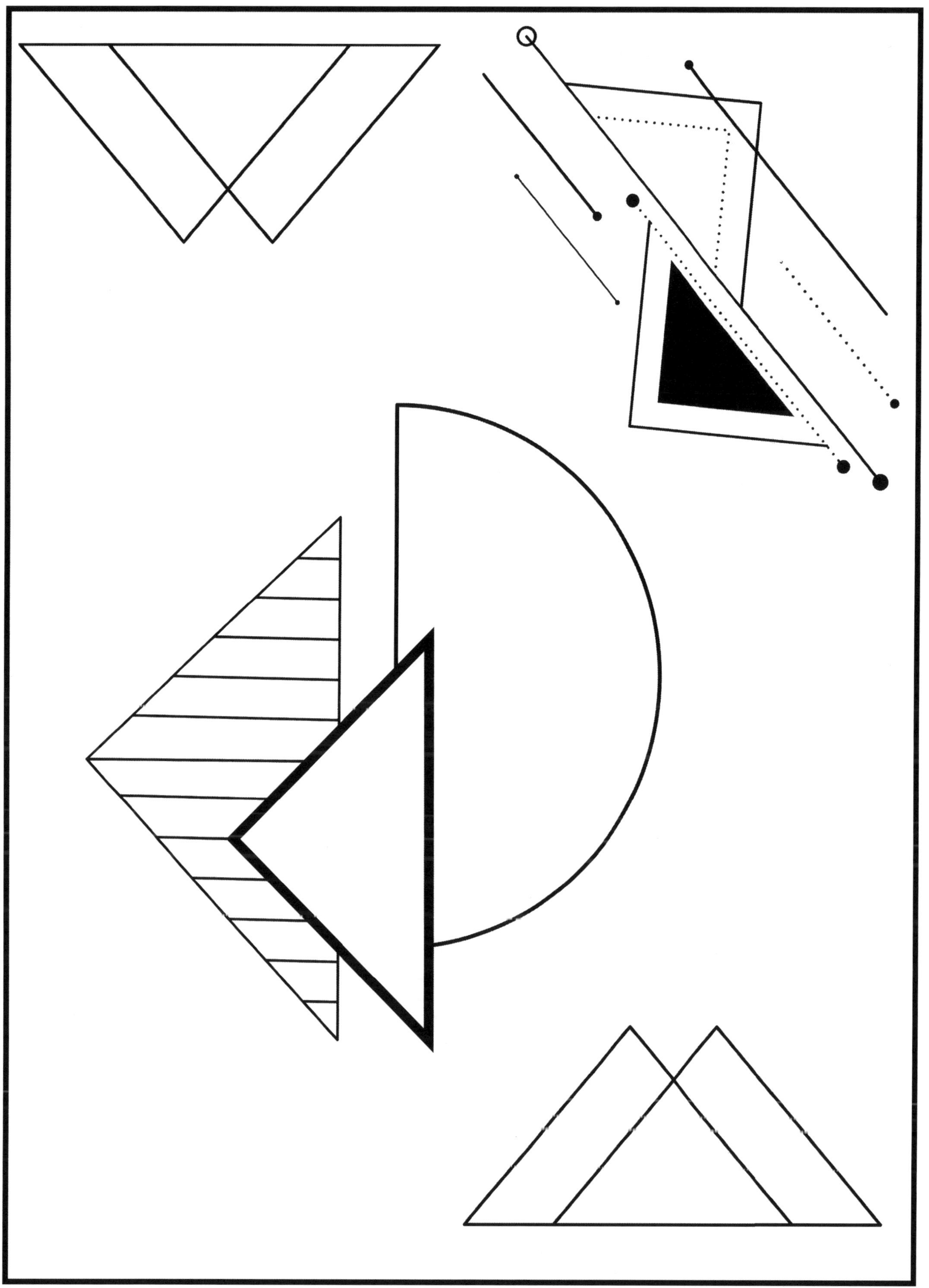

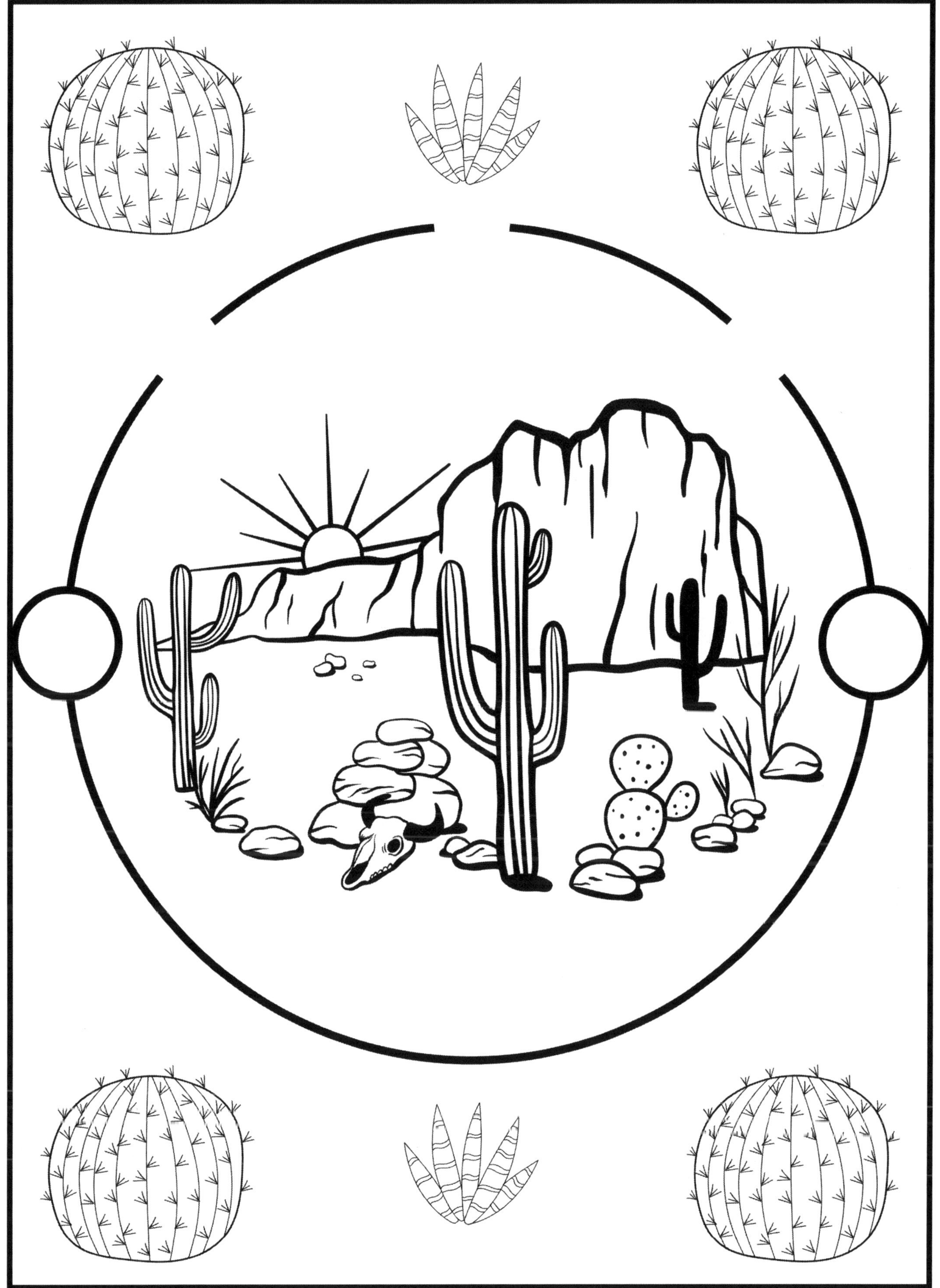

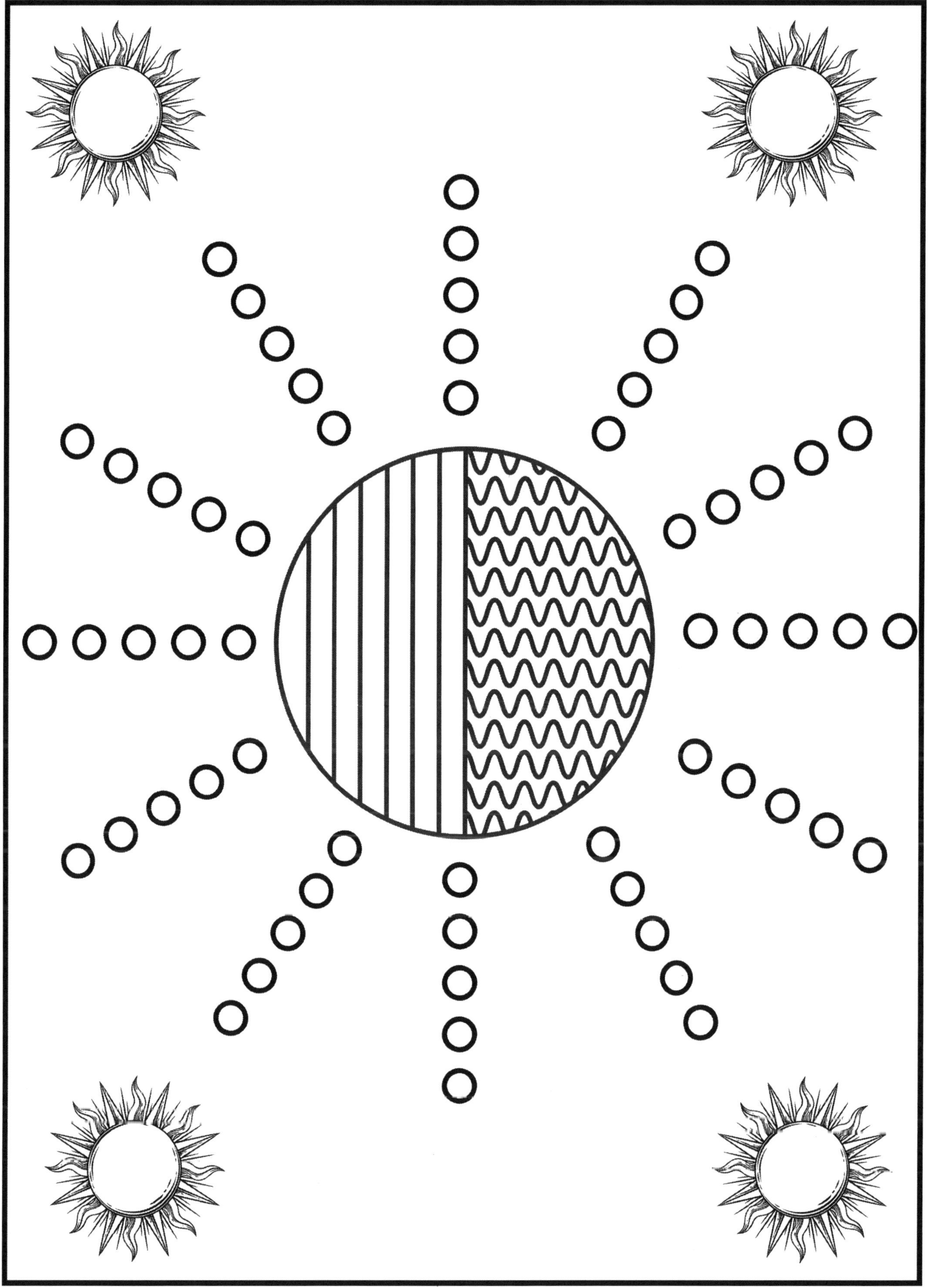

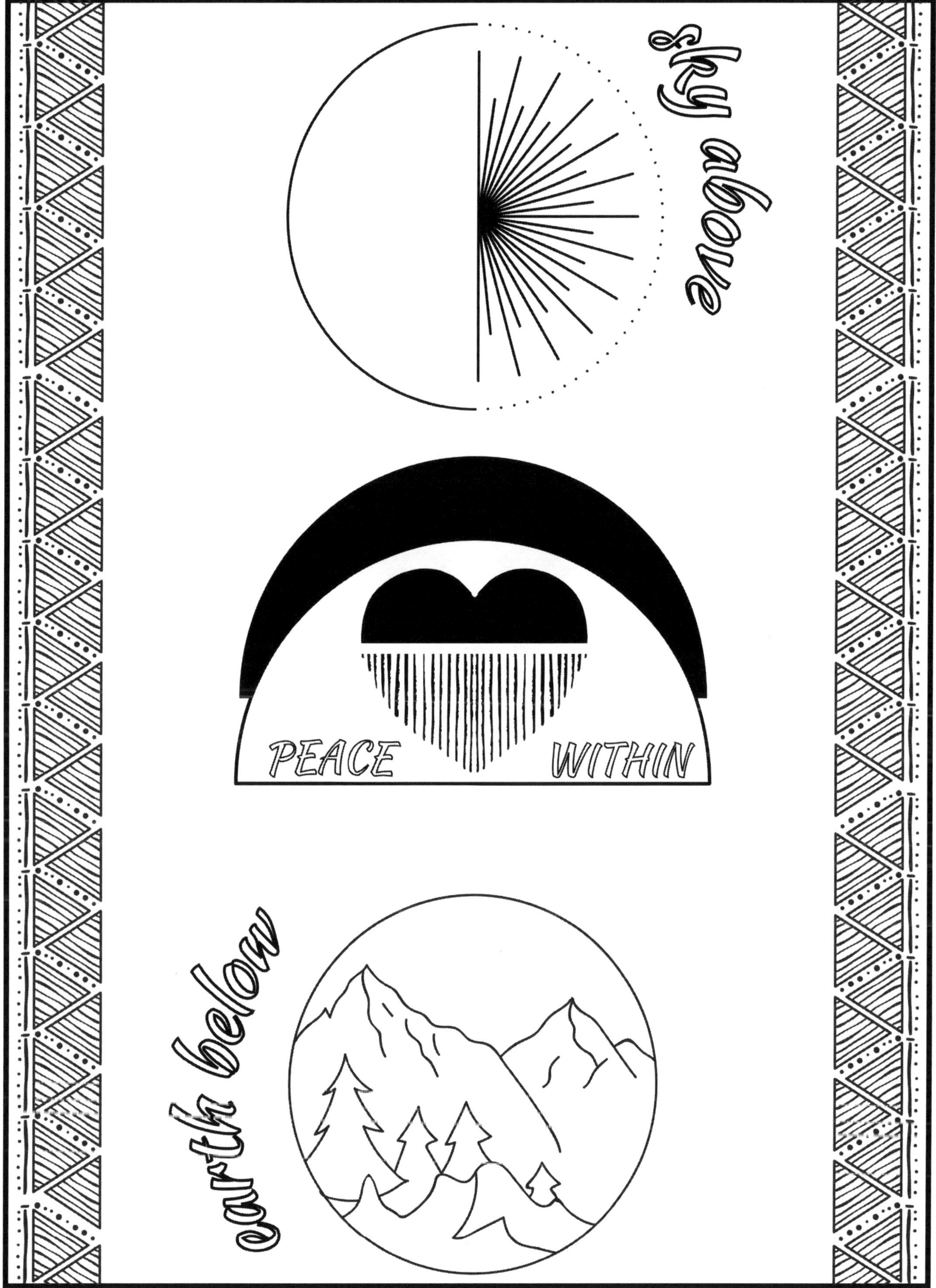

sky above
PEACE   WITHIN
earth below

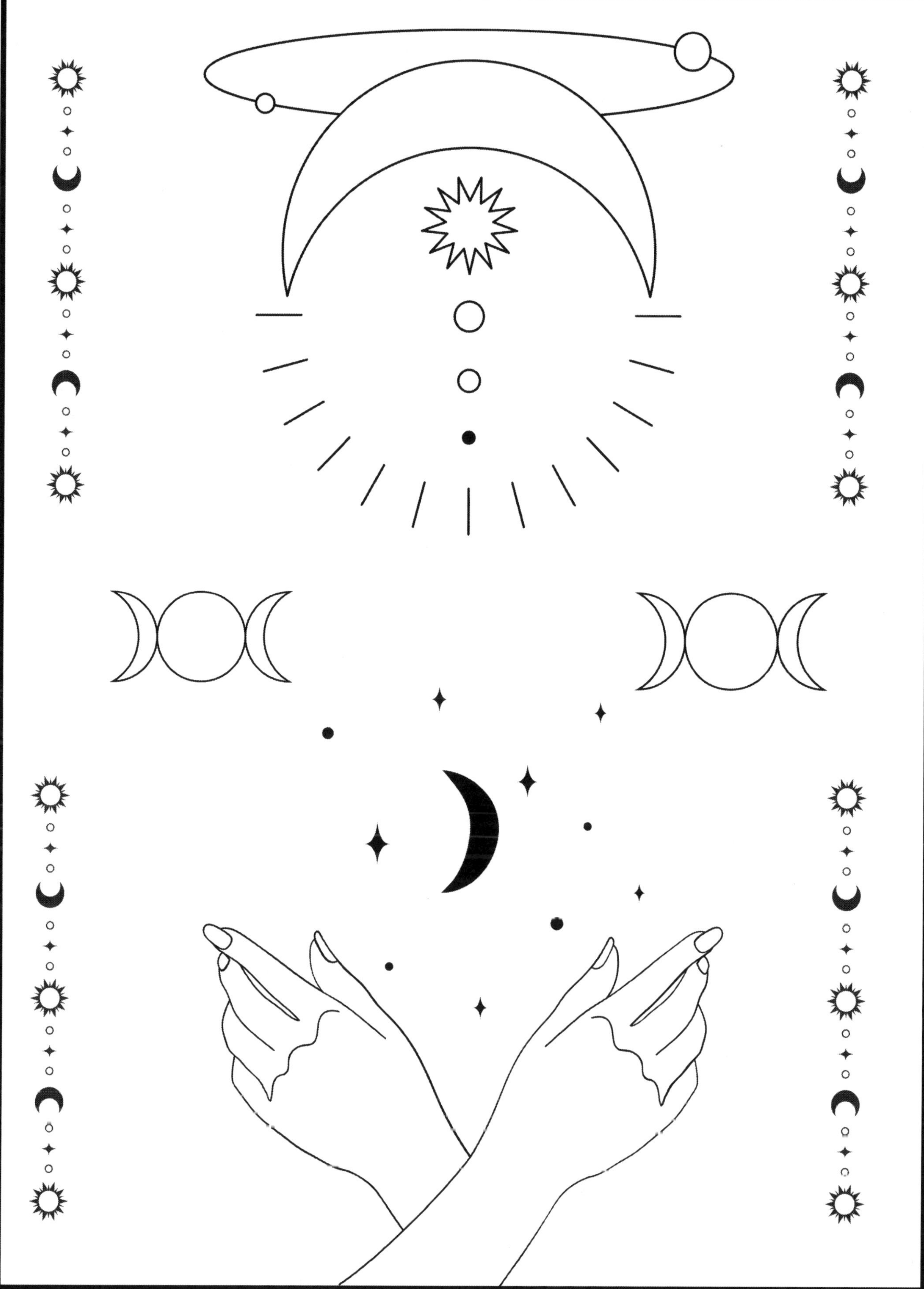

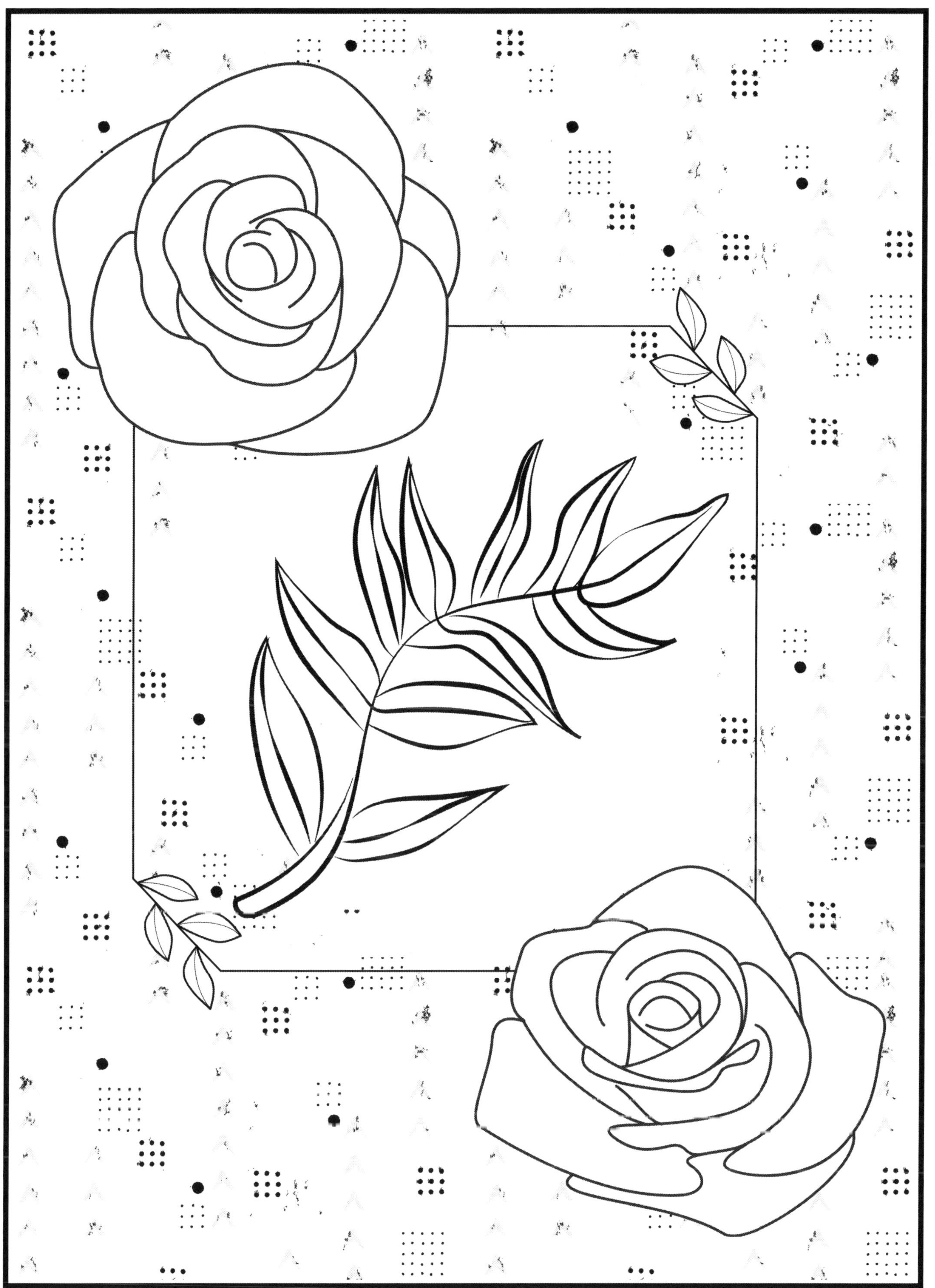

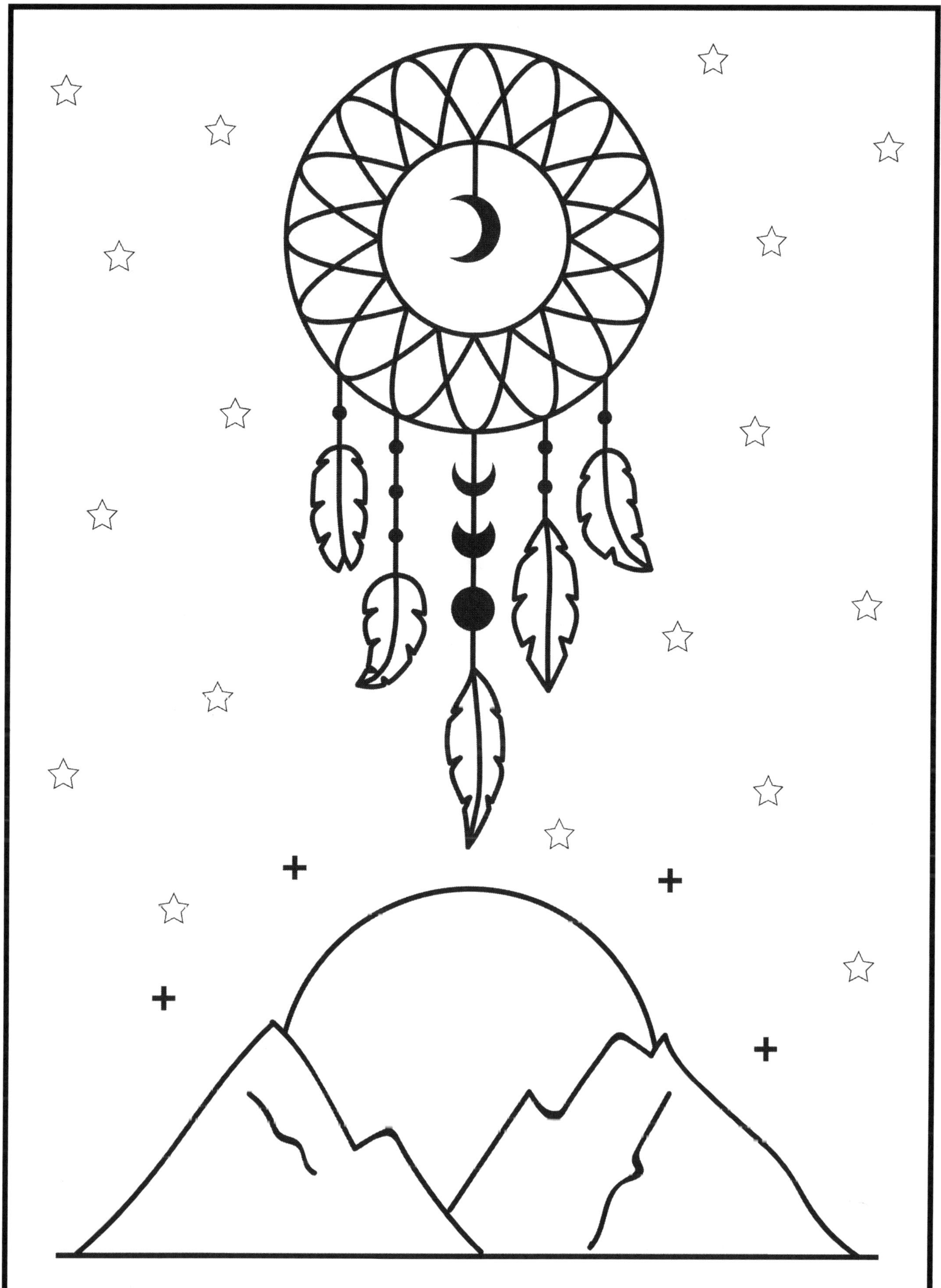

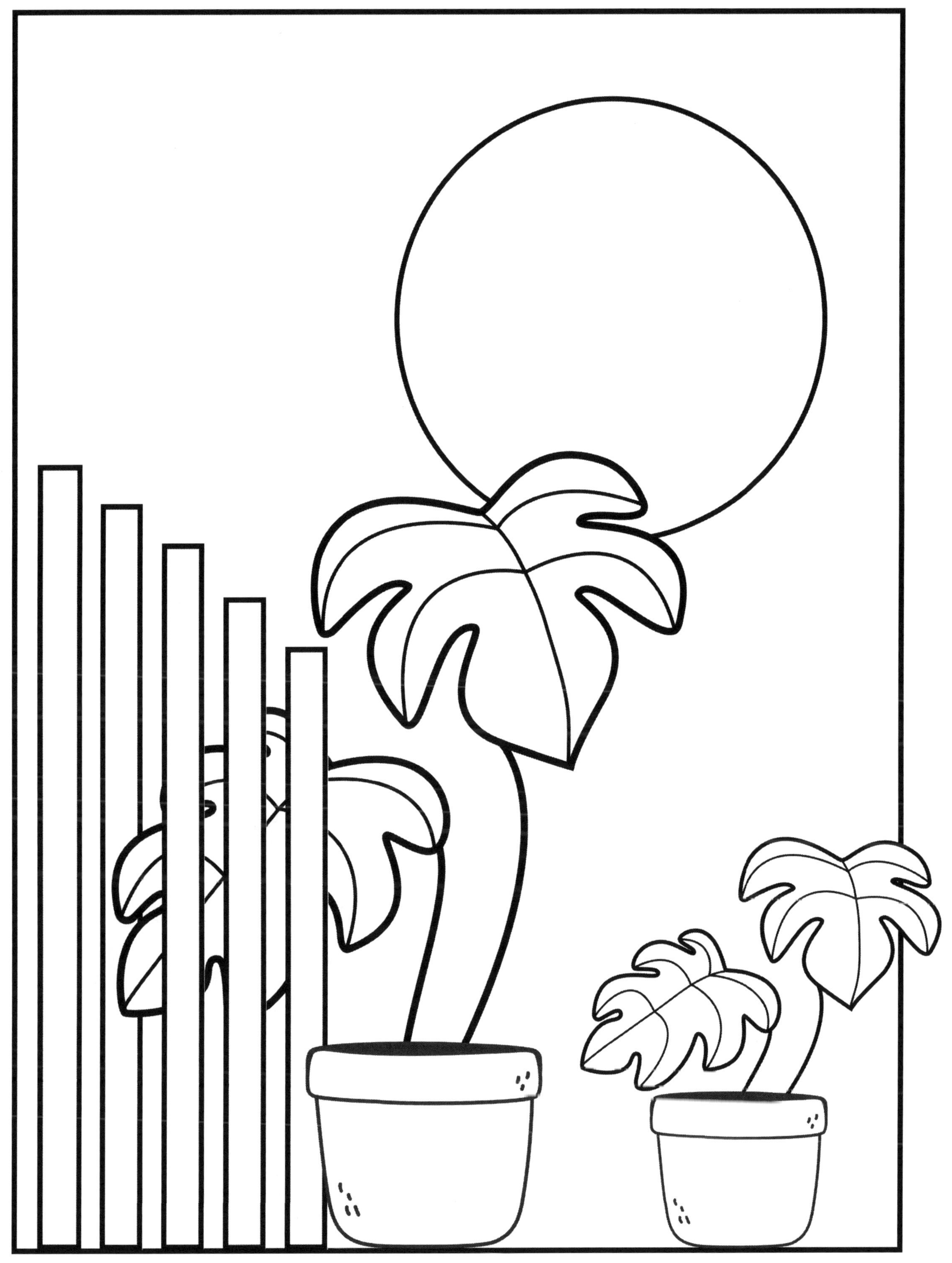

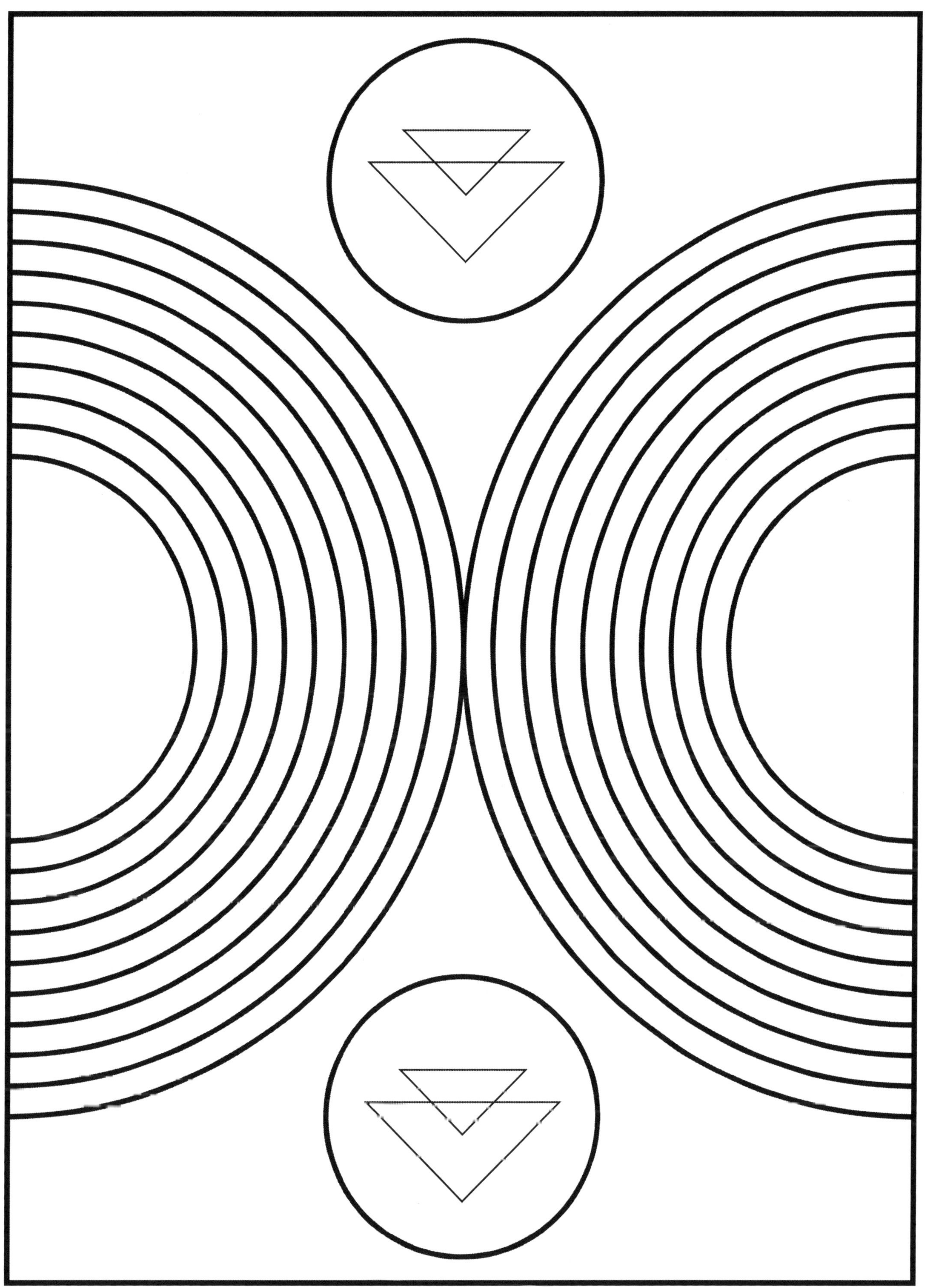

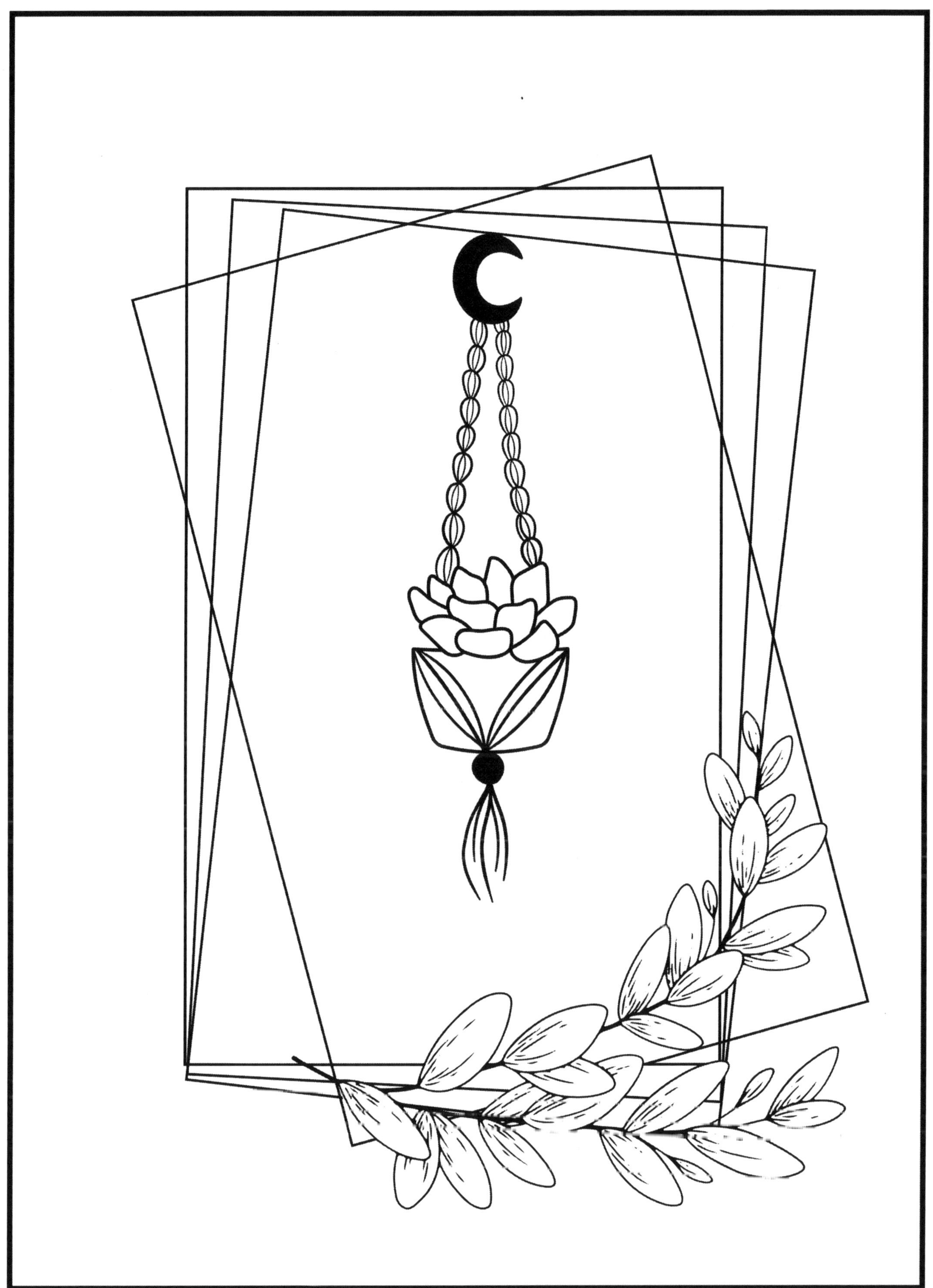

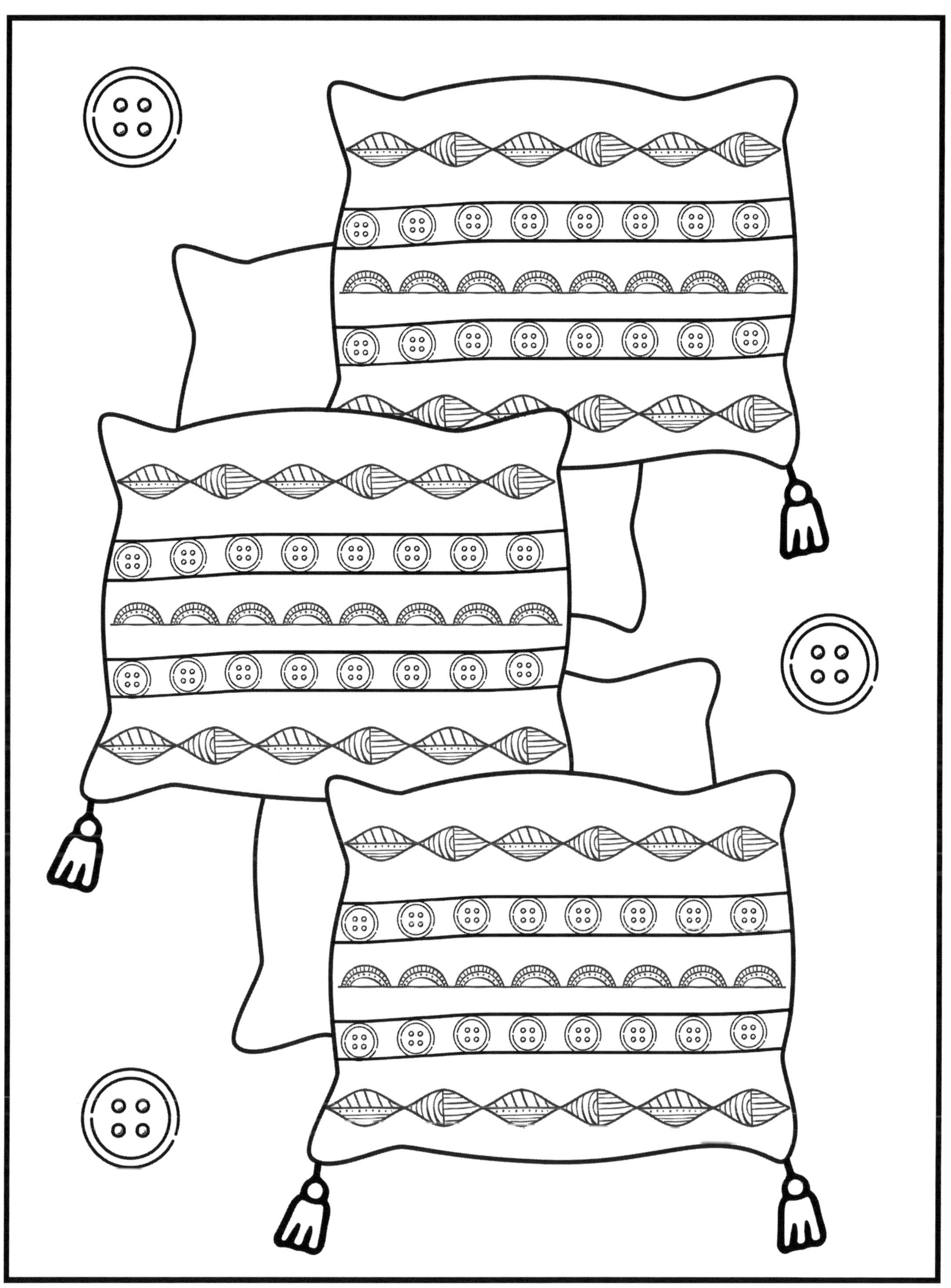

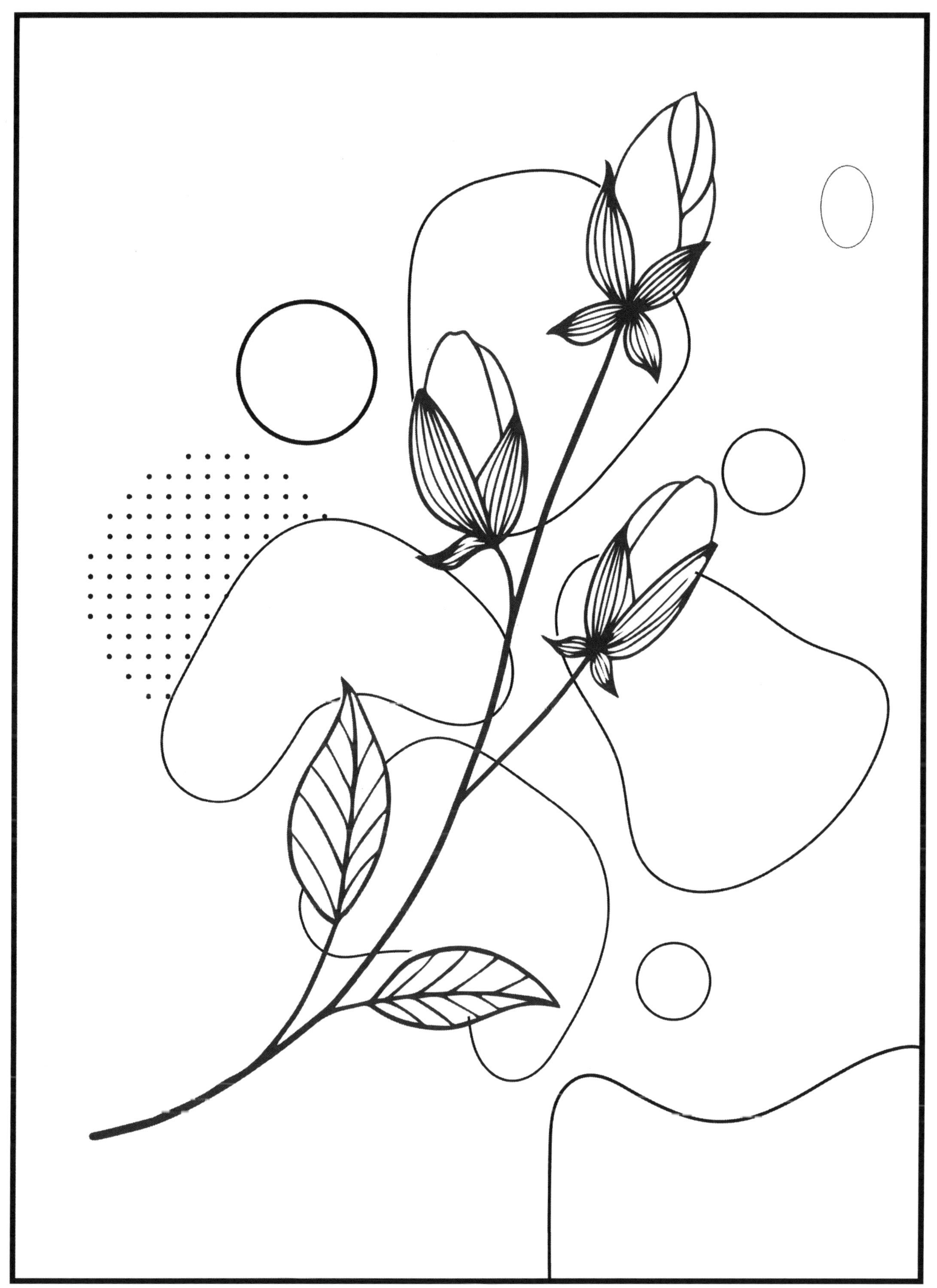

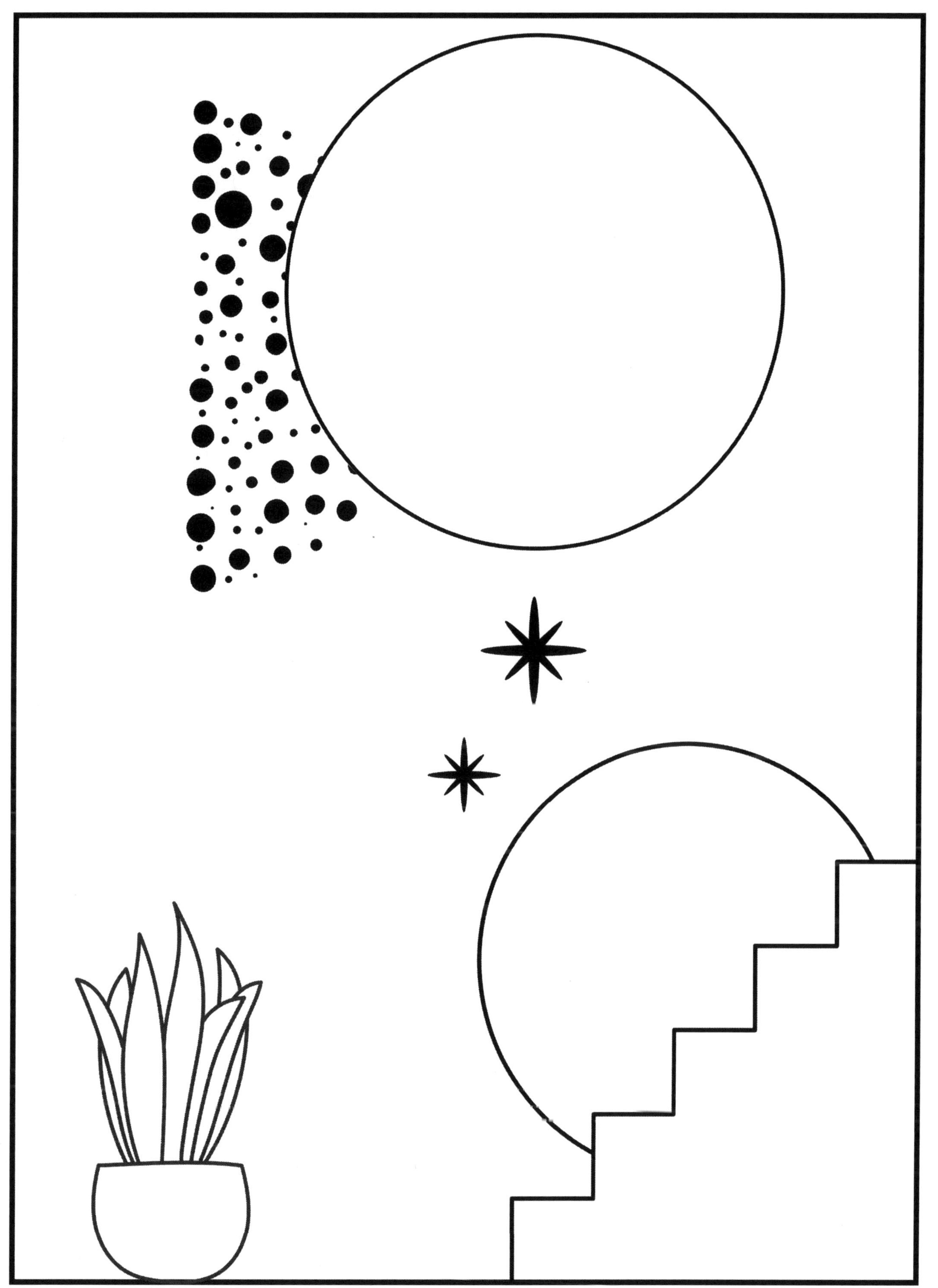

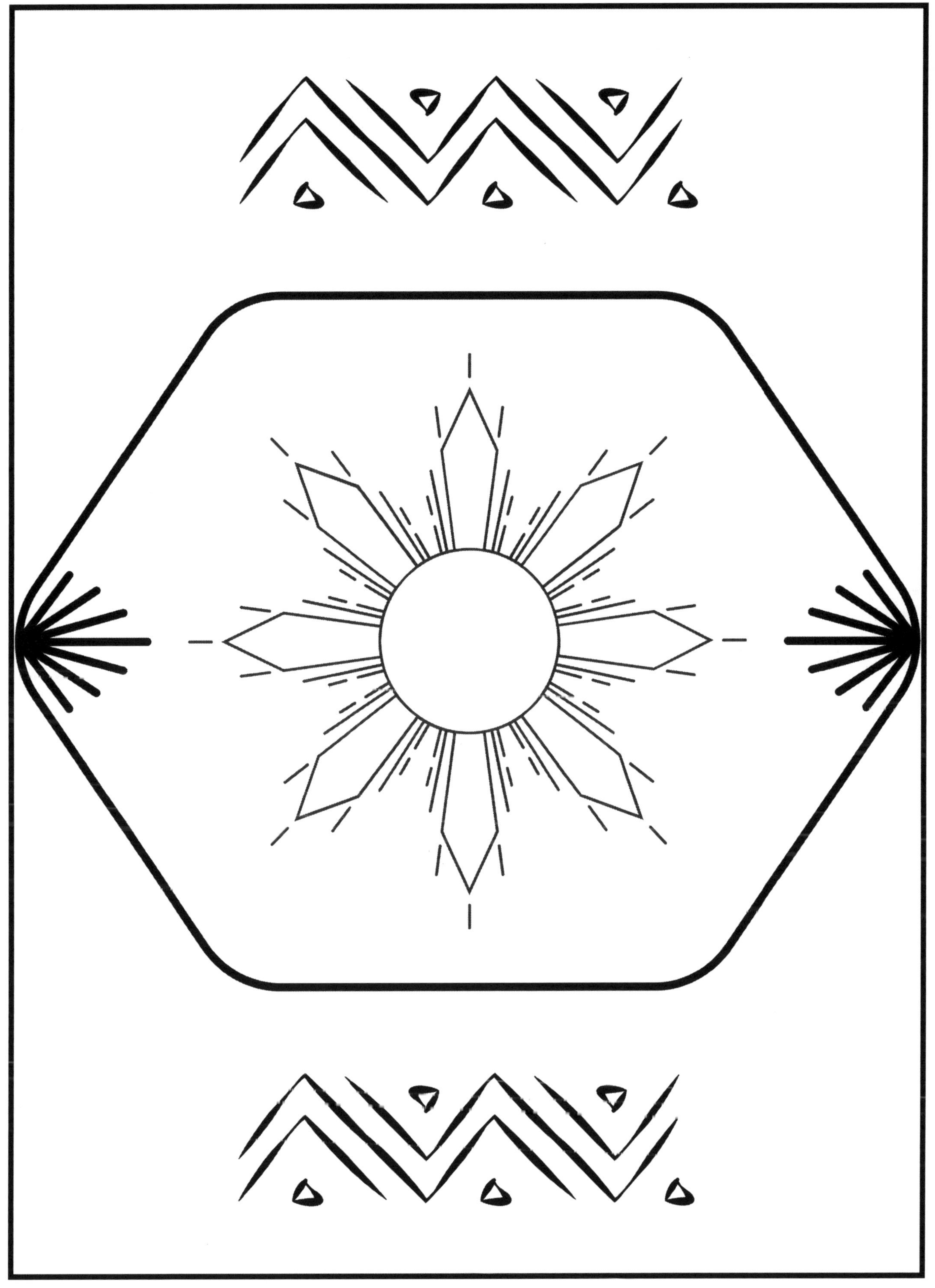

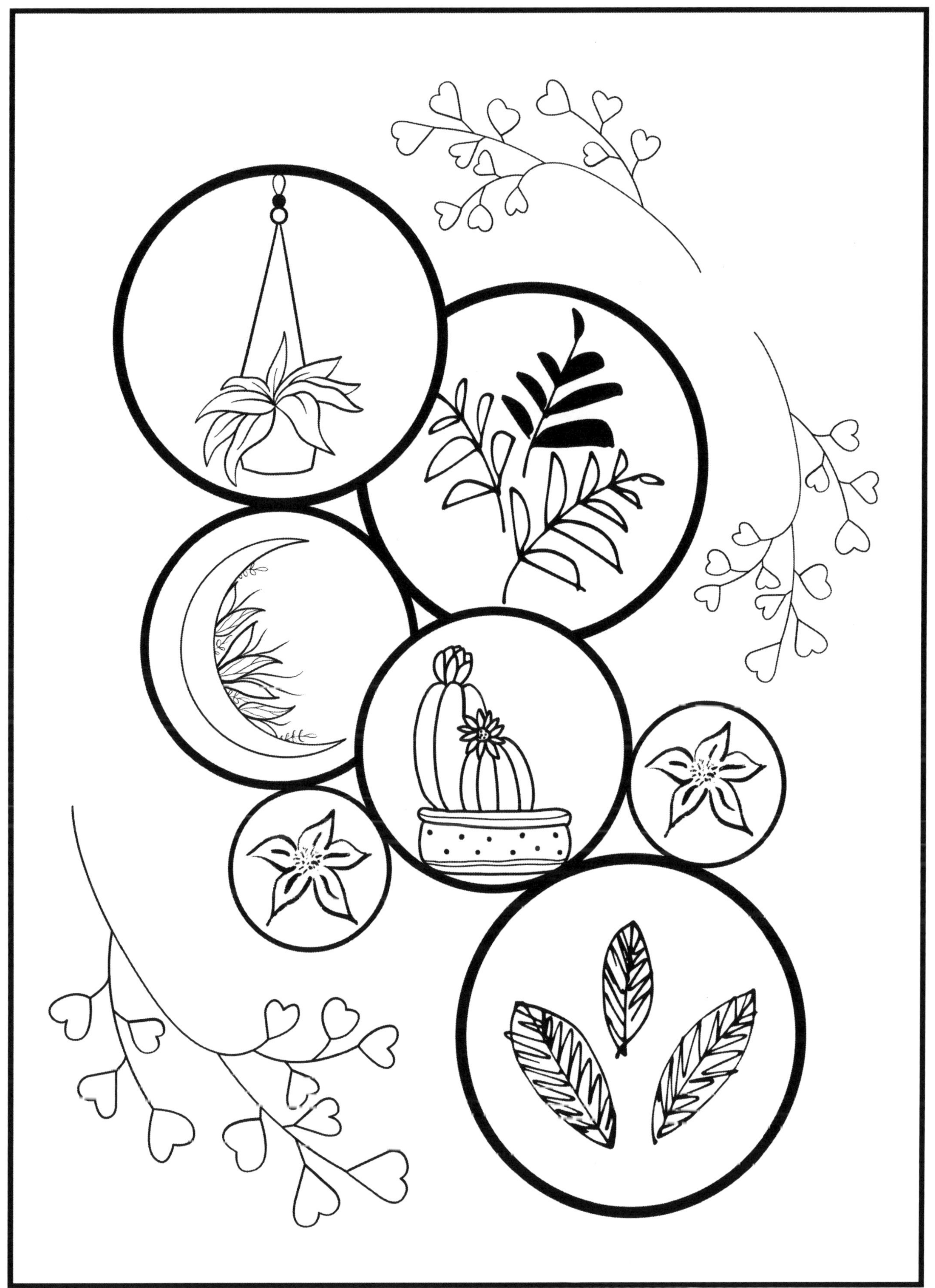

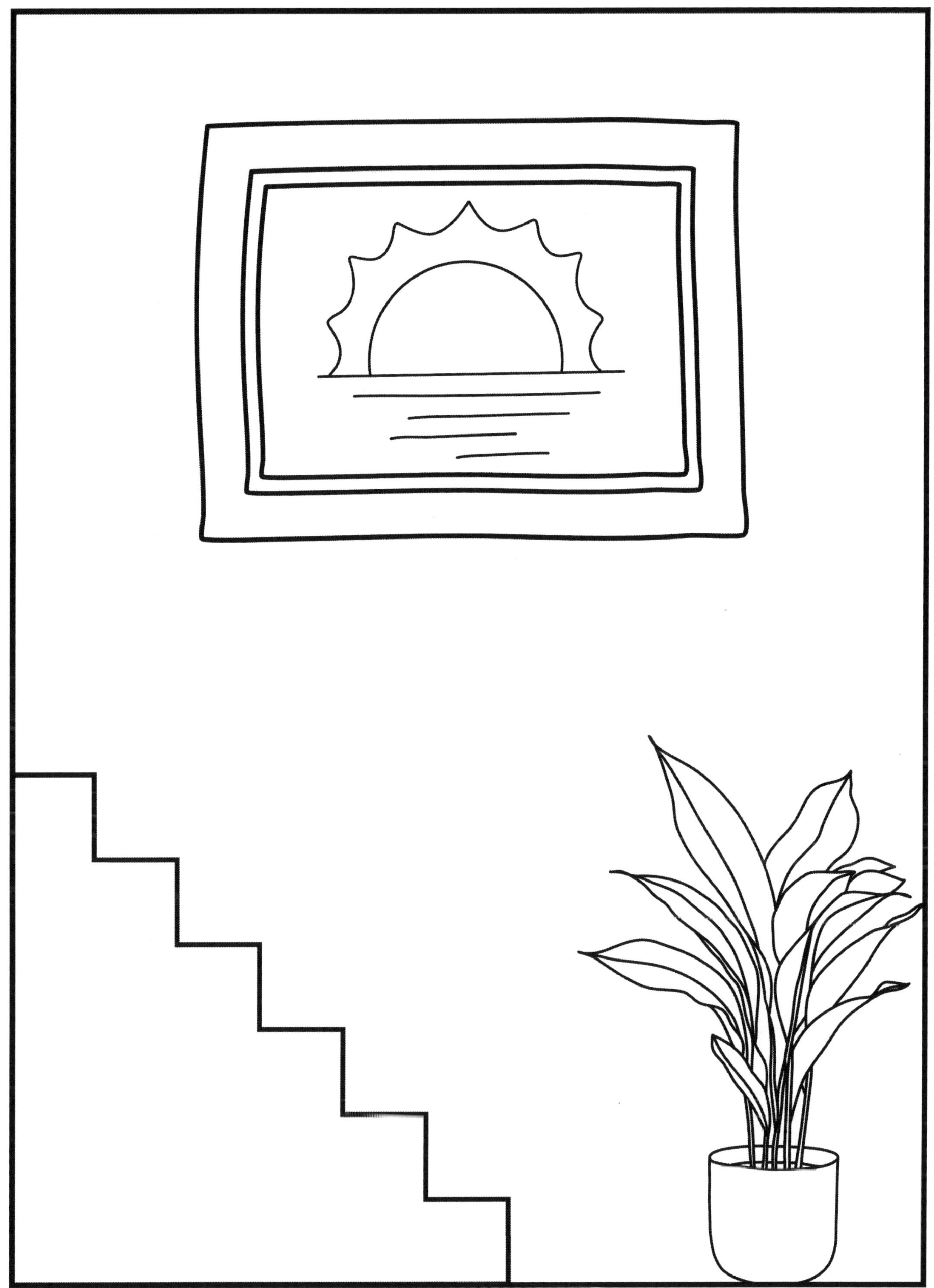

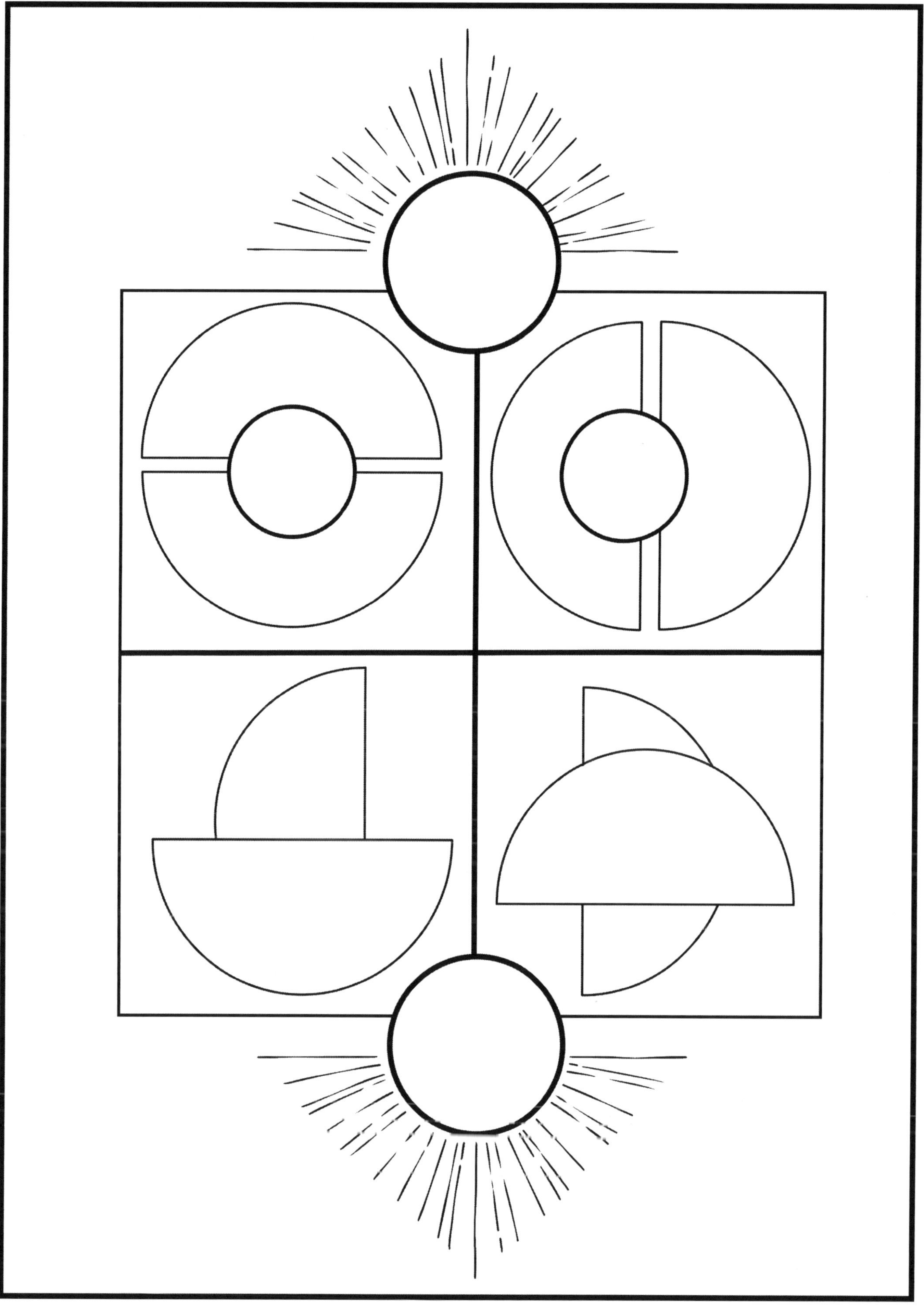

Made in the USA
Monee, IL
07 July 2026

56548191R00046